DIVING COZUMEL

DIVING
COZUMEL

By Steve Rosenberg

Aqua Quest Publications, Inc. ▪ New York

PUBLISHER'S NOTE

The Aqua Quest *Diving* series offers extensive information on dive sites as well as topside activities.

At the time of publication, the information contained in this book was determined to be as accurate and up-to-date as possible. The reader should bear in mind, however, that dive site terrain and landmarks change due to weather or construction. In addition, new dive shops, restaurants, hotels and stores can open and existing ones close. Telephone numbers are subject to change as are government regulations.

The publisher welcomes the reader's comments and assistance to help ensure the accuracy of future editions of this book.

Good diving and enjoy your stay!

Library of Congress Cataloging-in-Publication Data

Rosenberg, Steve, 1948-
    Diving Cozumel / by Steve Rosenberg.— 2nd ed.
        p.   cm.
    Includes index.
    ISBN 1-881652-31-9 (pbk.)
    1. Scuba diving—Mexico—Cozumel—Guidebooks. 2.
    Cozumel (Mexico)—Guidebooks. I. Title.
GV838.673.M6R67 2004
797.3'3—dc22

                                2003018216

Cover: Palancar Reef offers an endless number of swim-throughs and overhangs lined with lush corals and sponges.

Title page: The splendid toadfish, also known as the Cozumel catfish, is found in abundance on the shallow reefs of Cozumel.

Second Edition
Printed in China
10 9 8 7 6 5 4 3 2 1

Design by Richard Liu
Maps and line art by Justin Valdes
All photographs by the author unless noted

ACKNOWLEDGEMENTS

Thank you to all who contributed their time, effort and assistance in writing and illustrating this book.

I greatly appreciate the help and cooperation of my old friends Tim and Patti Massimino at the Scuba Club Cozumel.

I would like to thank Darlene Tarantino, her son Christopher Tarantino, her daughter Jessica Jovan, my daughter Shannon Rosenberg, and my other buddies Roger Hess and Greg Bassett, who have been assistants, models, sherpas and friends throughout this project. In particular I would like to thank Paul Padilla Perez, who always went out of his way to provide useful information, find unusual critters (including seahorses and batfish), lend a hand, and be a good friend. I would also like to thank German Yañez Mendoza of Yucatech Expeditions for his assistance with diving the caves of Cozumel.

A special thanks to Professor Bruce Heyer, a research biologist with the University of California for the information on Cozumel's oceanography.

Thank you to Jesse Cancelmo, Lisa Rooney-Zarri, Phil Zarri, and Patrick Rooney for allowing me to use a few of their slides to fill in the gaps. Thank you to Ignacio Cureño, Director of the Foundation of Parks on Cozumel and Cristina Doporto.

Finally, thank you to the many wonderful guides I have had the opportunity to dive with over the years.

CONTENTS

FOREWORD

Like countless other divers, my first warm water dive trip was to Cozumel. Since that first visit some 23 years ago, I have returned to the island an average of once a year, either on photography assignments, or to lead dive groups and teach seminars.

Many things have changed over the years, some good and some bad. Fast boats now make the southern sites more easily accessible. There has been a major amount of new construction, adding greatly to the commercialization of the island. Much of the new development is related directly to the cruise ship trade. A new country club including a golf course has been constructed at the northern end of the island. In the process, a large section of the mangroves that provided refuge and protection to great numbers of juvenile fishes was destroyed. Fortunately there has been little change in the excellent quality of diving; and the warmth of the people and the atmosphere remain the same.

Cozumel has a year-round pleasant climate, warm clear water, friendly people, plenty of topside attractions, and some of the best diving in the entire Caribbean.

The island is especially known for its exceptionally clear, 150-foot (46 m) visibility and for its effortless drift diving. The lush reefs on the southwestern end of the island offer incredible drop-offs, pinnacles, and labyrinths of interconnecting caves and tunnels. In addition, the variety and abundance of marine life is exceptional. Photographers and video enthusiasts will find more friendly, 'easy to shoot' reef fishes, eels and invertebrates than on any other Caribbean island destination.

Thirty-three of Cozumel's most popular dive sites, including shore dives, boat dives and cenotes are covered in detail in this guide . For all of the primary sites, a cross-section diagram is provided which shows the bottom profile and the depths of various points of interest. Also included is a chapter on Cozumel's interesting and unusual fishes and invertebrates.

There is also information on where to stay on Cozumel and suggestions on where to dine and shop. For those interested in exploring the island or the Yucatan Peninsula, there is a section devoted to the major points of interest, such as the extensive Mayan ruins and expansive beaches. Included are the small islands of Contoy and Isla Mujeres.

From beauty and excitement underwater to plentiful topside activities, Cozumel offers something special for every member of the family.

Steve Rosenberg
Fremont, California
June 2004

CHAPTER 1 ISLA DE COZUMEL

The Mexican island of Cozumel is located 12 miles (19 km) off the northeast coast of the Yucatan Peninsula. It is a small island—32.5 miles (52 km) long and 8.7 miles (14 km) wide —whose highest point is only 45 feet (14 km) above sea level. Cozumel is the largest of the three islands located off the northeast coast of Yucatan, the other two being Isla Mujeres and Contoy to the north. Cancun, on the mainland, is about 30 miles (19 km) northwest of Cozumel. Cuba is about 95 miles (59 km) to the northeast.

The reefs of Cozumel are part of one of the largest barrier reefs in the world, the Belizean Reef, that extends south from the tip of Isla Mujeres 174 miles (280 km) to the Bay of Honduras.

THE PAST

The pre-Hispanic history of Cozumel is closely tied to the rise and decline of Mayan civilization. The Maya established themselves in Guatemala 15 centuries before the birth of Christ. Their culture and influence spread quickly throughout southern Mexico. By A.D. 200 they were building cities on the Yucatan Peninsula. The Mayan civilization was at its peak between the seventh and ninth centuries.

The Mayans, who originally inhabited the island, referred to it as Ah-Cuzamil-Peten. In their language this meant "Place of the Swallows," so named because of the great numbers of swallows and other birds that once nested there.

Beginning in the tenth century, the Mayan civilization began to decline. Their numbers were greatly eroded by famine, pestilence and incursions by the warlike Toltecs from western Mexico. By the twelfth century, the Toltec cult of Quetzalcoatl, meaning 'Plumed Serpent,' dominated the Mayan culture.

In 1518, the island was accidentally visited by Don Juan de Grijalva, who landed in Cozumel with four vessels bound for Cuba. The number of well constructed stone streets and buildings amazed him. At that time, the island was very prosperous and well populated. The following year Spaniard Hernan Cortes discovered the religious center and renamed it "Santa Cruz De Cozumel." He remained on the island long enough to desecrate the Mayan's temples. It is believed that Cortes was offended by the idolatrous rites and ceremonies he witnessed. Therefore, he ordered his men to tear down the idols and erect a statue of the Virgin Mary in their place. Consequently, few of these impressive structures exist on the island today.

Cortes used the island as a staging area for his initial assault on the Mexican mainland. After the influx of the Spaniards and the spread of smallpox, the population on Cozumel had dropped from the 40,000 reported by Cortes in 1519 to less than 300 by the year 1570.

In the late 1600's, the island became a refuge for many pirates, among them the well-known Jean Lafitte and Henry Morgan. These experienced sailors appreciated the safety and protection offered by the leeward side of the island against violent storms. The pirates obtained fresh water from the lagoon at Chankanaab. They created general havoc with their drinking and fighting, disrupting the lives of the small population of Spaniards and Mayan Indians on the island. By 1843 the island of Cozumel was almost totally abandoned. In 1848, refugees from the turmoil

Bright red torch ginger flowers grow readily in the tropical climate of Cozumel.

on the mainland began to resettle the island.

Cozumel again became a center of activity when the chewing gum industry began to flourish in the United States. For centuries, the Mayan people had been satisfying their thirst by chewing raw sap from the zapote tree that grows on Cozumel and throughout much of Central America. In the early 1900's, the developed world was introduced to this new sweet treat, bringing a short-lived economic boom to the mainland coast. The new shipping routes included Cozumel, which has one of the best harbors in the area suitable for large ships. A few companies made large fortunes from the nickel pack of chewing gum, while the Indians who hacked their way through the dense jungle to tap the trees struggled for a subsistence. Partly because of this search for chicle, magnificent ruins were uncovered deep in the forested jungles on the mainland, and to a lesser extent on the island of Cozumel itself. Synthetics, which are now used almost exclusively in the manufacture of chewing gum, eventually replaced the hard-to-get chicle.

During World War II, the United States built an airstrip on Cozumel and operated a submarine base. During this period, special diving teams came to the island to train before embarking to the European and Pacific theatres of war. These divers began to spread tales of the incredible visibility and majestic underwater reefs around the island.

After the war, the island returned to relative obscurity until 1961 when a television documentary produced by Jacques Cousteau introduced the wonders of the reef to the public. Cousteau declared that Palancar and the surrounding reefs were among the most beautiful in the world.

The great pyramid of Uxmal, located south of Merida, is a good example of Mayan construction during the Classic Period. The ruins found throughout the Yucatan Peninsula are a silent reminder of the early history of Cozumel.

The Present

Since statehood in 1974, Quintana Roo, which includes Cozumel, has enjoyed a steady growth in tourism. By 1970, the population on the island had reached 10,000. Today there are over 100,000 people living on Cozumel, and some estimates suggest the population is even greater.

During the last few years, commercial development continues to increase at an astounding pace. New piers have been constructed and today over a million and a half tourists from cruise ships visit the island annually. A golf course now covers much of what used to be mangroves at the north end of the island. There is a large modern mall on the southern side of San Miguel. Additional shopping complexes are sprouting up around the heavily used cruise piers. Hopefully, this trend will cease to increase or at least slow down in the near future and the island of Cozumel will not grow into a high-rise city like Cancun because the island's water supply is already hard pressed to support the existing population. In addition, everything used or consumed on the island has to be shipped across the channel that separates Cozumel from the mainland.

Useful Information

Banks, Currency and Exchange Rates. Banks in San Miguel are open six days a week usually from 9:30 A.M. to 1:30 P.M. and longer when cruise ships are in port. Most resorts can provide pesos in exchange for United Sates currency, and have posted rates and times exchanges may be made. However, some resorts will not always be able to provide this service. The exchange rate is adjusted daily. While exchange rates are usually best at banks, the rate at hotels is not usually much less. The current exchange rate at the time of printing was approximately 9.5 to 10 pesos to the U.S. Dollar. Mexican paper money comes in denominations of 500, 1,000, 2,000, 5,000, 10,000, 20,000 and 50,000 pesos. Coins come in denominations of 5, 10, 20, 200, and 500 pesos.

It is no longer necessary to exchange American dollars for pesos. Virtually all commercial enterprises on the island accept U.S. dollars. While almost everyone will accept dollars, U. S. coins are rarely accepted by any of the local merchants, including taxi drivers.

Climate. Because Cozumel lies only 11.25 miles (18 km) off the Yucatan coast, it reflects a more continental climate than the oceanic dominated islands of the eastern Caribbean. The warm, humid jungles of the mainland trap solar energy during the day and release it at night which keeps the evenings warm. As the night progresses and the land continues to cool, the surrounding warm sea buffers any extreme drop in air temperature. Thus, Cozumel enjoys warmer days than islands further offshore and warmer nights than on the mainland.

Average annual temperature is about 80°F (27°C). During the mid to late summer months, temperatures can reach the low 90's F (about 33°C).

The rainy season begins in June and often lasts through October. During this period, it may rain daily and humidity is higher than during other periods. However, the frequent afternoon showers are usually brief. From November through May, it is generally balmy with lower humidity and an occasional cool evening.

In the winter months from December through February, cold fronts sweeping across the North American continent from the northeast can cause occasional overcast conditions and drop in air temperatures to 72°F (22°C).

Dining and Night Life. The warm, balmy evenings of Cozumel offer a variety of exciting nighttime activities. Every visitor should sample the food at some of the excellent restaurants, stroll among the lights and sounds of San Miguel, and pop into one of the dance clubs. Carlos N' Charlies and Senior Frogs, located on Avenue Rafael Melgar at the new Langosta Plaza at the south end of San Miguel, are among the established "happening places" to go for refreshment and fun.

Electricity. The electricity at most resort hotels is 110 volt/60 cycle, the same as in the United States. While voltage spiking once presented a serious problem, the output at most hotels seems constant and no longer a source of concern. However, if you have any worry about potential damage to electronic equipment, such as rechargeable strobes and chargers, use a voltage meter to test the output of the electrical sockets. If the current is over 120 and your charger is only meant to accept 110 volts, charge your batteries or battery packs for several short intervals, rather than for the recommended charge time. In any event, monitor the charger to see how fast it heats up. Don't let it get hot to the touch, or you may damage the electronic components.

Entry and Exit Requirements. A passport is required to obtain a tourist card to get into Cozumel. Children traveling with one parent need a notarized permission letter from the other parent. You will be issued a temporary Mexican Tourist Card upon departing the United States or on the plane flying into Mexico. The tourist card will then be stamped when you go through immigration at the airport after you land. Retain this document because it must be presented upon departure. Departure taxes are usually incorporated into the price of airline tickets. These taxes are payable at the airport after you check your bags at the counter, when not included in price of the ticket. The approximate amount of the tax is U.S. $10.00. If you enter Cozumel by international carrier, you must go through immigration, pick up your luggage and then clear customs. When you leave Cozumel, expect to have every piece of your luggage thoroughly inspected. Leave plenty of time for this delay at the airport.

The airport on Cozumel is about 1.9 miles (3 km) from downtown San Miguel. Whether you come to Cozumel by international carrier or domestic airline, stop off at the transportation desk to purchase a ticket for transportation to your hotel or resort. The rates are posted on the wall behind the counter for hotels in given areas. The fare is approximately US $3.00 for hotels in San Miguel, and US $6.00 to US $10.00 per person for hotels and resorts outside town.

You will receive a receipt from the clerk which you should then give to your taxi or mini-bus driver as soon as your bags are stowed in the vehicle. Make sure that all your bags are loaded before you leave the airport and make sure they all get off with you at your destination. On Cozumel luggage porters are eager to help you transfer your bags to the waiting taxis and US $.50 to $1.00 per heavy bag is a reasonable fee.

In addition to traveling by air, there are frequent, fast ferry trips between Cozumel and Playacar and Playa Del Carmen on the Yucatan mainland. Also, large cruise ships routinely visit the island, off loading swarms of eager shoppers and snorkelers.

Getting There. There are a number of international air carriers serving the island, including AeroCaribe, Mexicana and Continental. Domestic flights also arrive daily from the Mexican mainland. AeroCaribe schedules connecting flights from Cancun International Airport several times a day.

Island Driving. Driving around the main part of the island is easy. The island is flat and the roads are well cared for. A new, wide main road circles the southern two thirds of the island.

San Miguel is the only town on the island of Cozumel and it has grown substantially in recent years. There is a wide selection of restaurants and an endless number of souvenir, clothing, jewelry and department stores. The Plaza del Sol, located in the center of town along the shore road, has a number of modern civic buildings. The plaza affords a meeting place where townspeople gather for festivals, celebrations or friendly chats. The streets that immediately surround the plaza are closed to vehicular traffic, making it a pleasant area to stroll and watch the goings-on. Long time visitors to Cozumel will be amazed to see no fewer than six escalators installed in the downtown area.

In San Miguel, the roads are laid out in a grid pattern. The roads running north and south have the right of way, and you must yield or stop at all intersections when driving on roads running east and west. There are also many one-way roads. The shore road in San Miguel is named Avenida Rafael Melgar. This main road is also referred to as the Malecon or seawall. The main roads running parallel to Avenida Rafael Melgar in a north/south direction (parallel to the coast), are avenidas (avenues) numbered in increments of five. Avenida Benito Juarez is the main road running east to west. This road becomes the Cross Island Highway at Avenida 65. All numbered avenues on the south side of Avenida Benito Juarez are designated Sur (south) while those on the north are designated Norte (north).

The main roads running east to west in San Miguel are designated as Calles (streets). Calles are even numbered on the north side of

The paved roads on Cozumel are all flat and easily explored by moped or car. Rentals can be arranged through your hotel or resort.

Street merchants are found throughout downtown San Miguel, selling fresh fruit, fast foods and souvenirs.

Avenida Benito Juarez and odd numbered on the south side of Avenida Benito Juarez.

Avenida Benito Juarez begins adjacent to the Plaza in San Miguel by the passenger ferry dock and cuts straight across the middle of the island.

There are now two gas stations on the island. One is located at the corner of Benito Juarez and the other is located on the corner of Juarez and 75th Avenue. These stations are open from 7:00 A.M. to midnight everyday.

Driving in Cozumel is on the right side of the road, passing is on the left. All the speed limits, distance markers and speedometers are in kilometers. A kilometer equals 5/8 of a mile or conversely, a mile is equivalent to about 1.6 kilometers.

Rental Vehicles. If you want a little more freedom, or if you want to explore the outlying areas of the island, you may want to rent a vehicle. Before renting a vehicle, you must be able to show the rental agency your driver's license, a passport and a major credit card.

Rates vary greatly, but are approximately US $50.00 to US $80.00 per day. Collision insurance, which only covers 80 percent of any damages incurred, is well worth the additional cost. Be aware that in Mexico, your American car insurance is not valid. Curbs painted yellow are for bicycles and motorcycles/mopeds only. Curbs marked red are no parking zones. Never carry more than five persons in a vehicle.

When renting a vehicle, try to get one early in the day. There is a big difference in the quality of cars or mopeds that are available. Always inspect the vehicle thoroughly before you take it and have the agent write down any dents, scratches, missing equipment, and broken or non-operating windows. Check to see that the car is running properly, including forward and reverse gears, lights, brakes and horn. Also, make sure that the tires are not bald, and insure that there is a good spare tire and a jack. Jeeps, Volkswagens and compact sedans are the most common passenger rental

Beautiful sunsets are a common attraction on Cozumel's west coast. Many visitors to the island enjoy a relaxing evening, strolling along the beaches or swinging leisurely on seaside hammocks.

cars on the island. Most of the rental cars are two-wheel drive, so you should not travel over rugged terrain, especially the very bad roads at the north end of the island. A great way to explore the northeast side of the island is by 4-wheel ATV's, available from "Wild Tours" located near Mezcalitos on the east side of Cozumel.

Shopping San Miguel. There are many things to do in San Miguel. Most visitors take a break from diving and relaxing to spend at least a couple of hours shopping. Cozumel's most concentrated shopping area centers around San Miguel's Plaza Del Sol, in an area which now extends about 16 blocks along the waterfront and for several blocks back into town. The new 'Plaza Punta Langosta' is a new shopping mall located at the south end of town

across the street from the Punta Langosta cruise ship pier. There are also two large shopping areas near the cruise ship piers south of town (Muelle International T.M.S. and Muelle Puerta Maya). Cozumel is a duty-free port, and therefore offers many bargains. Of course, the best bargains you will find are on native merchandise, such as arts and crafts for which Mexico is famous. Among the most sought after items are clothing, jewelry (silver and semi-precious gems), Mexican liquor and souvenirs. Bargaining with vendors is no longer a wide spread practice on the island, and established stores will not dicker at all on their marked prices unless business is slow (after cruise line tourists have returned to their ships) or they are advertising a sale.

Black coral, tanzanite, lapis, turquoise and

silver are available in a wide assortment of unique and beautifully handcrafted jewelry designs and at very reasonable prices.

Most of the shops and boutiques offer the standard variety of souvenirs. A few of these shops have unique or sizable collections. There is no end of jewelry stores with high quality silver earrings, necklaces and pendants, including Van Cleef's in the Plaza del Sol mall and Tiffany's at Calle 2 Norte #9. Cinco Soles, located on the waterfront 4 blocks north of the ferry pier, has a wonderful selection of pottery, embroidery, paper mache creatures and other Mexican crafts. Among the best places to find marine jewelry and gifts are the shops located in the Villa Mar Plaza, close to the new downtown cruise ship pier.

Siestas and Business Hours. Cozumel still observes the traditional Mexican custom of the afternoon siesta during the heat of the day. For most shops, business hours Monday through

Saturday are usually 8:00 or 9:00 A.M. to 1:00 or 2:00 P.M., reopening at 4:00 or 5:00 P.M. until 8:00 or 9:00 P.M. Of course, when cruise ships are in port, most shops stay open throughout the day to take advantage of the surge in business patrons. Also, siesta hours don't apply to most eating establishments, which open early and stay open until 10:00 or 11:00 at night.

Taxis. Getting around Cozumel is fairly easy for visiting divers. Most visitors rely exclusively on taxis or simply walk between destinations. Taxis are closely controlled in Cozumel, so that the rates between given destinations are the same. Unfortunately, the rates are expensive. If you have a group, share taxis to reduce the expense. By law, standard taxis can carry a maximum of five passengers.

Always ask the driver for the quantity (*quanto*) of money the ride will cost before you get into the taxi. Technically, the drivers

Among the most popular items tourists shop for is silver jewelry.

should strictly adhere to standard rates, but there are often special circumstances when you may get charged a little more than usual.

Getting a taxi is no problem in most parts of Cozumel. If you are in a heavily trafficked area, all you have to do is stand on the sidewalk and wave at the first empty taxi that goes by. In town, taxis line up along the shore road in the middle of town and take passengers in order. Also, any hotel will be happy to call a taxi for you.

Time Zone. Cozumel is in the Central Time Zone and does not observe Daylight Savings Time.

Water. Turista, also know as Montezuma's Revenge, is a common worry among visitors to Cozumel as well as the other areas of Mexico. This illness is certainly no fun. It can cause uncomfortable cramping, chills, nausea, diarrhea, fever, dehydration and an overall fluish feeling. It is believed to be caused by, among other things, a strain of bacteria that often shows up in water or on uncooked food that is washed in unpurified water. Because the bacteria must get inside you to do the damage, consuming water or drinks that have ice cubes or eating fruits and vegetables washed in unpurified water are common ways to ingest the bacteria.

With a few precautions and by using a sensible approach to what you eat and drink, you can be fairly certain that you will avoid this unpleasant condition. The water is safer on Cozumel than on various other parts of Mexico because most of the water is well water. Also, most of the hotels and resorts are now serving purified drinking water and ice made from purified water. In some of the larger resort

The waterfront boulevard, Avenida Rafael E. Melgar, extends for twelve blocks along the downtown area. Many restaurants and jewelry shops are located along this road.

The "shark" greets visitors to the Villa Mar shopping area in San Miguel.

hotels, even the tap water is drinkable because they have their own desalinization systems.

However, to be safe, keep the following in mind:

■ Get bottles of purified water to keep in your room for drinking and brushing your teeth. Drink one or two quarts of purified water every day to prevent dehydration.
■ When you have water with your meals, ask whether the water is purified. When you have drinks with ice, make sure that the ice was made with purified water.
■ Use common sense when you go out to eat. If you eat vegetables or salads, they are not always washed in purified water. Fruit with thick skin that must be peeled is safe. Cooked foods are usually safe because the cooking kills the bacteria.

One should also keep in mind that a drastic change in diet often causes some of the same symptoms. What is often thought to be Turista is just your body's way of saying "enough" to too much fresh fruit, spicy food or other things that you don't usually eat or drink.

CHAPTER II ACCOMMODATIONS

The newer and more modern hotels and resorts are located on the shore or across the street from the water, and are either north or south of the town of San Miguel. Most of these hotels offer on-site bars, restaurants, pools, air-conditioning, palm-shaded beach areas, and either on-site dive shops or diving activities provided by one of the excellent independent dive operators.

Hotels in the town of San Miguel are generally less expensive as they are located away from the shore. They are, however, within easy walking distance of cafes, restaurants, shops and the main Plaza. There is a fairly wide diversity of rooms available. Some of these are small and sparsely furnished, while some are luxurious, and offer such additional amenities as central courtyards, restaurants, bars and comfortable gathering places or meeting rooms. Most have private baths. Some hotels and condominiums also offer rooms with kitchens. These facilities can be a great bargain for families or close-knit groups. Almost all hotels have ceiling fans and/or air-conditioning.

Normally, rates for all hotels and resorts are higher from the middle of December through Easter week. A 10 to 15 percent room tax is added to all quoted rates for hotels.

A note on hotel beaches. Most hotels on Cozumel have access to a beach for swimming and sunning, which is indicated in the hotel box which follows. Some of these beaches are large and sandy, and slope down into the water. Others may simply be a stretch of sand above the ironshore bank with steps going into the water. In addition, while most hotels are close to the water, some are across the street from the water. In this case, you may have to cross the road (usually via a tunnel or bridge) to access the beach. If a large, sandy beach is important to you, be sure to ask your travel agent or dive center what type of beach a resort has. Remember that all of the beaches on Cozumel are open to the public.

To telephone Cozumel from the United States, add **011-52-987-87** before the five-digit local number.

Small schools of grunts can be found on most of the shallow reefs in Cozumel.

Scuba Club Cozumel is one of several excellent resorts that cater primarily to divers.

	Rooms/Units	Air Conditioning	Tennis	Beach	Pool	Restaurant	Bar	Dive Operation	Gear Storage
North of San Miguel									
Club Cozumel Caribe Tel: 20100	220	■	■	■	■	■	■	■	■
Coral Princess Hotel Tel: 23200, 25122	139	■		■	■	■	■	■	
El Cozumeleno Beach Resort Tel: 20050	252	■	■	■	■	■	■	■	
Paradisus Cozumel Tel: 20411	147	■	■	■	■	■	■	■	■
Playa Azul Hotel Tel: 20033	50	■	■	■	■	■	■	■	
Sol Cabanas Del Caribe Tel: 200411,200412	252	■	■	■	■	■	■	■	
Downtown									
Bahia Suites Tel: 24034	27	■							
Baracuda Hotel Tel: 21243	52	■		■		■	■	■	■
Casa Mexicana Tel: 20209	90	■			■			■	
Colonel Suites Tel: 20506	28	■							
Cozumel Costa Brava Tel: 21453	24	■							
Presidente Inter-Con. Tel: 20322	253	■	■	■	■	■	■	■	
Reef Club Beach Resort Tel: 29300	240	■	■	■	■	■	■	■	
El Marques Hotel Tel: 20677	40	■							
Hacienda San Miguel Tel: 21986	11	■							

	Rooms/Units	Air Conditioning	Tennis	Beach	Pool	Restaurant	Bar	Dive Operation	Gear Storage
Hotel Del Centro Tel: 25471	14	■			■				
Palma Dorada Inn Tel: 20330	18	■							
Plaza Las Glorias Tel: 22000/22400	168	■		■	■	■	■	■	
Sun Village San Miguel Tel: 20233/20323	96	■			■		■		
Villa Del Rey (Days Inn) Tel: 21600	45	■			■	■	■		
South of San Miguel									
Allegro Resort Tel: 29770/23443	300	■	■	■	■	■	■	■	■
Casa Del Mar Tel: 21900	106	■		■	■	■	■	■	■
Costa Club Tel: 22900	180	■	■	■	■	■	■	■	
Fiesta Americana Tel: 22622	226	■	■	■	■	■	■	■	■
El Cid-La Ceiba Tel: 20844	113	■	■	■	■	■	■	■	■
Lorena Dive Resort Tel: 20188	22	■		■	■			■	
Safari Inn Tel: 20101	12	■			■				■
Scuba Club Cozumel Tel: 20663	95	■		■	■	■	■	■	■
Sol Caribe Tel: 20700	355	■	■	■	■	■	■	■	
VillaBlanca Tel: 20730	68	■	■	■	■	■	■	■	

CHAPTER III DINING

Cozumel has a wide assortment of places to eat ranging from elegant restaurants to fast food stands. You don't need directions to most restaurants; just give the name to the taxi driver. It is advisable to obtain reservations for dinner at the restaurants located in town, especially during peak season from mid-December through Easter. Reservations may be arranged by your hotel staff.

Many of the hotels and resorts have their own restaurants, some of which are excellent. At several hotels a package price is available that includes lodging, diving and meals. For example, the diving packages at the Scuba Club Cozumel includes meals. The restaurant at Scuba Club Cozumel has a wide variety of delicious and authentic Mexican dishes, as well as a few American offerings.

Most resorts and hotels, however, don't include all meals in their packages even though they have excellent restaurants. Many of the newer resorts boast more than one restaurant.

Many tourists who have been to Cozumel more than once have found favorites among the many wonderful restaurants scattered around the island. Listed below is a sampling of restaurants touted by visitors and locals.

Aquario Restaurant   21097

The Aquario is located at Avenue Rafael Melgar Sur #779 on the south end of San Miguel, about a half mile (.8 km) from the Plaza El Centro. The décor of this fancy restaurant mirrors the specialties of the house, which are fish, succulent lobster and prime rib dishes. Inside there are huge aquariums filled with a variety of Cozumel's brightly colored reef fishes and sharks. Outside and behind the restaurant there are open ponds full of interesting marine life.

Fonda Viejo Cozumel   26735

Fonda Viejo Cozumel is a small restaurant tucked away off the beaten track at the corner of Avenida Sur at Calle 7. Each night there is a tempting dinner special produced by the owner David Guerro. Among the house specialties is a nice selection of inexpensive yet fantastic examples of traditional Mexican cuisine. The menu is limited but enticing. Many visitors in the know list this small eatery as one of a handful of Cozumel's very best.

Prima Trattoria   26567/22477/24242

Prima is located at 109 Avenida A. Rosada Salas just behind the main Plaza El Centro. Prima specializes in northern Italian cuisine, offering classic dishes such as shrimp tortellini, lobster ravioli, and crab and spinach manicotti smothered in creamy alfredo sauces. There is also an extensive selection of fresh grilled seafood, prime rib, veal, and vegetarian dishes. All pasta is handmade daily along with daily fresh baked breads. Fresh desserts made daily include chocolate peanut butter mud pie, gran marnier tiramisu and spumoni. This rooftop, garden setting restaurant has been highly acclaimed by several of the leading travel guides.

Morgan's   20584

This elegant and romantic dinner spot is in the main part of San Miguel on the north side of the Plaza. The specialties here are continental and Mexican dishes. The waiters make a flaming crepes suzette dessert which, when

Carlos N' Charlies is a famous bar and restaurant located on the waterfront. If you want to go where the action is, this is the place.

coupled with a variety of nightly musical entertainment, is one of the best after-dinner shows in town.

Pancho's Backyard   22141

Pancho's is located inside the Los Cinco Soles store at 8th Street, on the waterfront north of the main plaza. Its excellent Mexican cuisine is served on a patio lined with water fountains.

Guido's   20946

Pizza Guido's, formerly Pizza Rolandi, is located at Avenida Rafael Melgar #23 between Calle 6 & 8 North four blocks north of the Plaza on the waterfront. It is a favorite with most repeat visitors. Sit in the enclosed outdoor courtyard, and enjoy one of their excellent pizzas from the wood-fired oven, the Rolandi (calzone), or their delicious lasagna. Begin the meal with their unusual garlic bread, a puff flour tortilla made from pizza dough and covered with loads of garlic, and add a pitcher of very special sangria. Finish off the meal with one of their house-made desserts and a fresh mocha or latte.

La Cocay Restaurant   25533

La Cocay is located at the intersection of Ave. 25 and Calle 17 Sur number 1100. This cozy and relaxing restaurant specializes in Mediterranean cuisine. The tempting appetizers have included Greek salads, three-cheese oven dried tomato tarts, special house salads and mushroom stuffed tortellini with tomato ragout. The menus change monthly, but past favorites have included duck and seafood creations, seared sliced sirloin in a red wine mushroom sauce, or the almond and vanilla bean crushed fish of the day. There is seating both inside and outside, and the service is excellent. The restaurant offers wonderful desserts. They do not accept credit cards.

Ernesto's Fajitas Factory   21154/ 20145

Ernesto's is located on the beach at Carretera Sur Km 4 between the Aquaworld Pier and Atlantis Submarine. Ernesto's specializes in an assortment of tasty fajitas, including shrimp, chicken, and beef. The cooks prepare the fajitas with an entertaining flourish. Ernesto's is now one of the best places to go for breakfast on the island. Try their tasty eggs benedict.

The French Quarter   26321

The French Quarter is the place to go for a taste of Louisiana. The diverse menu includes crawfish appetizers, cajun sausage, hush puppies, deep fried mushrooms, Louisiana style gumbo and jambalaya, and prime black angus steaks and "all you can eat" ribs. The restaurant, located on 5th Avenue South, between Rosada Salas and 3rd Street (Calle) is a little piece of New Orleans with plenty of ambiance. Dining is in the downstairs air-conditioned dining room or upstairs under the big palapa. The downstairs bar is one of the "in" places to hang out for Monday night football. The service is excellent.

La Veranda   24132

La Veranda is a romantic restaurant located on Calle 4 North, 1° blocks off the waterfront, between 5th Avenue and 10th Avenue. Dine indoors or in the spacious but intimate garden patio. They offer an excellent selection of entrees including San Miguel Caribbean fish, margarita shrimp, flaming shrimp Caribbean, shrimp curry, jerked chicken or lobster prepared by their master chefs. Start the meal off with one of their excellent appetizers. This is a favorite location for weddings and anniversary parties.

Carlos N' Charlies   20067

The infamous Carlos N' Charlies has moved to Rafael E. Melgar #11 on the waterfront in the new Punta Langosta Plaza. Carlos N' Charlies has been a Cozumel landmark for over a decade as the "in" night spot, with a party atmosphere. It caters to an all ages crowd. Though not considered a formal restaurant, you can get great appetizers, burgers, BBQ ribs and a good assortment of Mexican and American food. It has always been a great place to let go, have fun, and people watch. It is located beneath a newer hot spot— Senior Frogs which caters to a younger set.

Morgan's Restaurant is a romantic dinner spot on the north side of the Plaza El Centro.

Chankanaab Reef has an unusually large number of spiny lobsters prowling the interior caves and tunnels of the reef.

CHAPTER IV SIGHTSEEING

COZUMEL

The Foundation of Parks and Museums offer many exciting attractions and activities. Besides the museum, they operate the archaeological sites, Chankanaab Park and Punta Sur Park.

Archaeological Sites

Certainly the most interesting and most extensive archaeological site on the island is the **San Gervasio** Mayan ruins. These ruins have undergone extensive excavation and restoration, and the Park Foundation now offers very interesting guided tours. The site covers over 10 acres (4 ha) and is located at the end of a toll road approximately 6 miles (10 km) north of Avenida Juarez, east of San Miguel in the middle of the island. As you stroll beneath the tall trees and well manicured grounds, guides, fluent in English, give groups of tourists detailed historical information on the site and its Mayan inhabitants. A half day visit to these ruins is time well spent.

Another archaeological site is **El Cedral**, located at the end of a 2-mile (3.2 km) dirt road which leaves the shore road just south of San Francisco Beach. El Cedral is small in size, but it is the oldest Mayan structure on the island. A few traces of paint and stucco of the original Mayan artist still remain. It is believed that this ruin was once a major site. In the 1800's it was used as a local jail. A tree grows from its roof with thick exposed roots tangled in and around the stones of the ancient structure. Four-hour horseback riding tours are offered at **Buenavista Ranch** on the southeastern end of the island Monday through Saturday. This is a great way to explore many unexcavated ruins scattered over a large area of land. For more information call 21537 or e-mail to sunflower@prodigy.net.mx.

Chankanaab Park

Chankanaab Park, probably Cozumel's number one attraction after scuba diving on the barrier reef, has lots to do for everyone in the family. The centerpiece of the park is the **Chankanaab Lagoon**, which means "small sea" in Mayan. The park includes **dolphin encounters**, a **sea lion show**, **snuba**, **botanical gardens**, white sand **beaches** and, of course, **diving** and **snorkeling**. The **archaeological park** offers 60 exact replicas of stone art works from Mesoamerica. The lush botanical garden surrounds the lagoon and provides a beautiful and relaxing walk. The beach at the park is a great place to try water sports, nature encounters or just soak up the sun. The "very commercial" dolphin program gives visitors the opportunity to interact with dolphins.

Punta Sur Park

The **Punta Sur Park Ecological Reserve** covers more than 100 acres (41 ha) and offers a wide variety of activities. For visitors the park offers **catamaran trips** around **Columbia Lagoon** for sightseeing and **bird watching**, **crocodile and sea turtle workshops**, great **beaches**, ruins and the **Punta Celarain Lighthouse**. There is an incredible 360° view from the top of the lighthouse. Access to the park is U.S. $10.00 per person and the park is open 365 days a year. There is a small archaeological site **Tumba del Caracol** located on the east side of the access road to Point Celarain Lighthouse near the south end of the island. Directly across the road is an observation deck overlooking Columbia Lagoon, which usually offers views of resident salt water crocodiles.

Tulum is the site of a carved descending god, often referred to as the "diving god." Photo: Phil Zarri.

MUSEUM OF THE ISLAND OF COZUMEL

For a good understanding of Cozumel's natural environment and exciting history, be sure to schedule a visit to the Museum. The four permanent exhibit halls provide information of particular interest to divers. These include a relief map of Cozumel, showing the relative ocean depths around the island, and 3-dimensional displays of the reefs depicting varieties of fishes, corals and reef structures. There are also charts and models that reveal how the reefs were formed. Perhaps the most important reason for divers to visit the Museum is that it graphically points out the potential harm from careless divers.

The Museum is located on Avenue Rafael Melgar, $2^{1/2}$ blocks north of the Plaza between 4th and 6th streets. The telephone number is 21007.

A tourist poses with a trio of trained iguanas at San Francisco Beach.

San Francisco Beach offers a wide variety of water sports, including swimming, snorkeling, parasailing and jet-skiing.

The tall, white lighthouse at Punta Celarain is worth a visit. Ask permission to climb to the top for a beautiful 360 degree view of the surrounding area.

Workshops at Punta Sur Park

Catching and Tagging Crocodiles. Park personnel have recently started a conservation program to observe and record data regarding the population of crocodiles that inhabit the lagoons and mangroves at Punta Sur Park. Scientists working for the Park service have recently started catching, measuring and tagging the crocodiles. In only the first few months of the program, over 100 adult crocodiles had been tagged, the largest over three meters in length. A workshop is available for visitors on the island to accompany park personnel on these expeditions and witness first hand the nocturnal behavior of these wonderful animals. The cost of participation is $55.00 per person, with a minimum of two people, including water, refreshments, headlamps and life jackets. The outings involve the use of two small boats in the shallow waters of Columbia and Chunchacab Lagoons and take place at night usually between the hours of 8 P.M. and midnight. The program is available year round. A windbreaker is a good idea and mosquito repellant is a must!

Sea Turtle Nesting Sites. During the months of May through July, hundreds of female turtles deposit their eggs on the beaches of southeastern Cozumel. Between July and September, tens of thousands of turtle hatchlings are born within the boundaries of the Punta Sur Park. Park biologists monitor and supervise the behavior of these sea turtles. There are also daytime and nighttime workshops for visitors to the island. The workshops include an introductory video, a beach trek to the nesting areas and refreshments. The nighttime expeditions involve accompanying park biologists on their rounds. This is a great opportunity to learn about and observe unique behaviors in the wild. The cost for the nocturnal expeditions is $55.00 per person and the time runs roughly from 9 P.M. to 1A.M. Comfortable clothing and shoes are recommended, along with insect repellent.

The cost of transportation to Punta Sur is not included in the price of either workshop. For more information call the Park at 20914 or 22940 between the hours of 9 A.M. and 3 P.M. or visit their website www.cozumelparks.com.mx.

Scientists tag a five-foot (1.5 m) crocodile during the crocodile workshop.

The dolphin discovery program offers a variety of activities including diving and snorkeling with dolphins.

The guides working at San Gervasio offer a wealth of information about Mayan culture.

Beaches

Cozumel has some outstanding beaches for sunning, snorkeling and other water sports. All of the island's beaches are open to the public. Even the big hotels cannot, by law, restrict access to their beaches. On the east side facing the Caribbean Sea, quiet beaches alternate with rocky shores along the deserted coastline. The waters on the west side are generally calmer, while the heavy surf on the east coast creates serious breakers and very strong undercurrents.

Along the main road on the west side of the island, there are a number of "beach clubs" which are bars and water sports centers for tourists. These include **Playa Sol** and **San Francisco Beach**. San Francisco Beach, a two-mile (3.2 Km) long sandy beach which is mostly a hot spot for the non-divers, is located 10 miles (16 km) south of the center of San Miguel. There are several restaurants, bars, live music, para-sailing and an assortment of other water related sports. Some dive operations still visit San Francisco Beach or one of the nearby beaches to have lunch between dives on two-tank trips. Playa Sol is a Beach Adventure Park just south of San Francisco Beach. The water sport activities include parachute and banana boat rides, wave runners, sailboats, and water skiing, in addition to snorkeling and diving.

Although the surf on the east side of the island is very impressive, it is dangerous for swimming. **Playa Orienta** is a good beach at the end of the cross island road. There are several more beautiful, nearly deserted beaches along the east shore; **Punta Morena**, **Punta Chiqueros**, **Chen Rio** and **El Mirador**. Most of these beaches have small cafes and bars located on the beach. Punta Morena is clearly marked. Punta Chiqueros is a large crescent shaped beach. Chen Rio is only identified by a large outcropping of rocks that form a small bay, ideal for swimming and snorkeling. At the south end of the beach, where the road turns back west, you'll find El Mirador, a clean sandy shoreline with few rocks. The entire east side is an endless stretch of long, empty beaches, shells, and waves.

EXPLORING THE YUCATAN PENINSULA

The Yucatan Peninsula juts to the northeast from the southern tail of the Mexican mainland. The peninsula is bordered on the north and west by the Gulf of Mexico, on the east by the Mexican Caribbean and on the south by Belize, Guatemala and the neighboring Mexican State of Tabasco. The Yucatan Peninsula is composed of three different states: Campeche on the west, Yucatan on the north, and Quintana Roo on the east. With its beautiful beaches, lagoons and fabulous Mayan ruins, the peninsula has become an important drawing card for tourists.

Getting There

By boat. Passenger ferries depart regularly from the dock at the end of Avenida Benito Juarez in San Miguel. The new modern ferries hold many passengers in airline-style seats. The trip between Cozumel and Playa Del Carmen takes an average of forty minutes. There are 10 to 12 trips between Cozumel and Playa Del Carmen daily, leaving on the hour. Playa Del Carmen, located directly across the channel from Cozumel has grown from a sleepy village into a high-rise tourist mecca. Cruise ships come and go from the International Piers, two of which are located at the south end of hotel row (Muelle Int. T.M.S. and Muelle Int. Puerta Maya) and a third (Muelle Punta Langosta) at the south end of San Miguel. Car ferries depart the International Piers twice daily.

By air. There are several daily flights between Cozumel and Cancun, the newest and most modern international airport on the Yucatan Peninsula. The two domestic airlines are AeroCaribe and AeroCozumel. Both provide regularly scheduled flights between Cozumel, and Cancun, Merida, Playa Del Carmen, Isla Mujeres, Chetumal, Chichen-Itza and other destinations.

The Coast

The eastern coast of the state of Quintana Roo extends about 223 miles (360 km) from Cancun south to Chetumal. Throughout most of the year, the coastline resembles a tropical paradise of palm groves, low brush and mangroves. The jungle that lines the coast contains many lagoons and natural underground freshwater rivers. Stretches of long sandy beaches alternate with rocky promontories, inlets and small protected bays.

Mezcalito's is a popular bar on the east side of Cozumel, at the end of the Cross Island Road.

The waterfront on Isla Mujeres is lined with boats of every size and description. Some are used for ferrying tourists back and forth to Cancun, while others are used for diving and fishing excursions.

Cancun

The resort destination of Cancun is located near the northeast tip of the Yucatan Peninsula. In 20 years, it has exploded from a swampy area of land with a population of zero to a mega-bucks resort with over 200,000 people.

There are actually two different Cancuns. One is long, slender island connected to the mainland by a bridge at each end. This island is literally lined with wall-to-wall high-rise luxury hotels resembling massive, modern pyramids. Across the bridge at the northwest end of the "row" is Cancun City. Here, visitors will find moderately priced hotels and condominiums within walking distance of the sidewalk cafes and a multitude of shops. There are a number of shallow reefs located a short distance from the hotels, but because of the run-off, the visibility is generally not very good.

Isla Mujeres

Isla Mujeres is a small island, approximately 5 miles (8 km) long and ° mile (.8 km) wide, that lies 8 miles (13 km) across the Bay of Mujeres from Cancun and approximately 45 miles (73 km) north of Cozumel. The island is flat with large stretches of sandy beaches. There are fewer than 20,000 residents on the island, whose main town is a laid-back fishing village. Isla Mujeres has maintained its quaintness even though it has been discovered by tourists.

You can get there by plane or ferry. There

One of the attractions of diving from Isla Mujeres is the well-known "sleeping shark caves" on the northeast side of the island. Photo: Jesse Cancelmo.

are connecting flights from Cancun International Airport, as well as infrequent direct flights from Cozumel. AeroCaribe usually has three flights a week to Isla Mujeres, but the schedule is constantly changing.

There are two main ports where ferries leave from Cancun to Isla Mujeres. Puerto Juarez, located about 15 minutes north of downtown Cancun, is known as the "people ferry." This port has medium size ferries running at regular intervals throughout the day. Arrive at least 15 minutes earlier than the scheduled departure because the boats often leave a little early if they are full. You can also hire a small water taxi. These small boats are normally faster, however, depending on weather and water conditions, the ride can be wet and wild. There is also a "people and car" ferry that leaves from Punta Sam on a daily basis. The trip from Punta Sam is less frequent and longer. If you plan on staying on the island for only the day, be sure to check the last departure time

for the mainland.

There are a number of comfortable hotel accommodations on the island with a wide variety of prices. During peak tourist season, reservations are suggested. Isla Mujeres also has many excellent restaurants, sidewalk cafes, souvenir shops, fishing cruises, a market, banks, bakeries, pharmacies and dive shops.

You can also rent bicycles or hire taxis to get from one end of the island to the other. The town at the north end of the island is small enough to walk through unless you are hauling dive gear. The best beaches are **North Beach** on the northern end of the island near the town and **El Garrafon Beach** on the southern end of the island. El Garrafon offers the best snorkeling, but is often very crowded.

Isla Mujeres is the location of the well-known **sleeping shark caves** and also has some very interesting shallow dive sites. The caves of the sleeping sharks are located on the northeast side of the island and are accessible only when the ocean is calm. The various caves are between 50 and 70 feet (15-21 m) deep. Although the sharks are not always present, there is a good chance that divers will be able to see bull sharks, lemon sharks or gray reef sharks "sleeping" on floors of the caves.

Manchones Reef is a popular shallow reef on the southwest side of Isla Mujeres, off El Garrafon Beach. This large site offers a series of coral ridges in depths between 20 and 40 feet (6-12 m). The tops of the ridges are lined with elkhorn coral, and divers can expect to encounter large schools of grunts, snapper and goatfish hovering above sections of the reef.

Isla Contoy

An interesting side trip from Isla Mujeres is Isla Contoy, a bird sanctuary located about a 45-minute boat ride north of Isla Mujeres. The island is deserted, except for many varieties of exotic birds, a government owned museum and a lighthouse. The island also offers excellent snorkeling.

Tulum, meaning "wall" in Mayan, measures approximately 1,255 feet (380 m) by 545 feet (165 m). Tulum was part of a series of coastal forts established between A.D. 700 and A.D. 1000. Photo: Phil Zarri.

The tops of many of the reefs near Isla Mujeres, including Manchones, are lined with beautiful growths of elkhorn coral.

Chichen-Itza exhibits a mingling of Mayan and Toltec architecture, and is perhaps the most popular destination of its type on the Yucatan Peninsula. Photo: Phil Zarri.

One of the most interesting and graceful structures at Chichen-Itza is Caracol, the observatory. Photo: Phil Zarri.

Archaeological Sites

One of the most popular archaeological sites on the mainland is **Tulum**, located about 15 miles (25 km) south of **Akumal** on coastal highway 307. A side road leads to the ruins that cover an area 180 yards (165 m) by 435 yards (398 m). There are approximately 60 well-preserved stone structures at Tulum, which are perched atop a cliff overlooking the ocean. This is the largest fortified site on the Quintana Roo coastline.

There is a picturesque sandy beach situated below the cliffs offering a place for a refreshing swim after a tour of the ruins. Many divers who come to Cozumel for a week trip take a day excursion to Tulum. The tour can be arranged through your resort on Cozumel. Most people take the ferry, hydro-plane or travel by air to Playa Del Carmen and then continue on by guided taxi or bus tour. After a guided tour of Tulum, be sure to visit the natural lagoon of **Xel-Ha** for some snorkeling before continuing on to the beach resort at Akumal for a late lunch. Xel-Ha (pronounced shell-haah), has a beautiful lagoon that consists of a mix of fresh and salt water inhabited by some rare tropical fishes. The lagoon is now a national park and is protected from fishing.

The extensive ruins of **Chichen-Itza** are now only a one hour plane ride from Cozumel on AeroCaribe. The aerial view of the main pyramid and the lush green jungle is very impressive. This is the most famous of the ancient Mayan cities. The earliest buildings date back to A.D. 600. While most of the buildings are Mayan, those dating from the 10th century include a Toltec influence, resulting from the Toltec invasion which began around A.D. 950.

Among the most interesting features of the ruins at Chichen-Itza are the 75-foot-high (23 m) pyramid (a temple to Quetzalcoatl, named Kukulkan by the Mayans), the ritual ball courts where the winners were sacrificed and the El Characol observatory.

Coba is a site which dates back to the classic Mayan period. It is set among several lakes located inland from the coast about 60 miles (97 km) southwest of Cancun. This area was never discovered by the Spaniards and consequently has been found in an unspoiled condition. It is currently undergoing excavation and restoration. The site covers an

Coba is an island site that was never discovered by the Spaniards. Photo: Phil Zarri.

immense area of more than 19 square miles (50 sq km) and hundreds of mounds are yet to be cleared and uncovered. **Nohoch Mul**, which towers 12 stories above the ground and is the tallest pyramid on the Yucatan Peninsula, offers an excellent (and dizzying) view of the surrounding jungle and the remainder of Coba.

CHAPTER V DIVING

Almost all diving in Cozumel is done along the leeward western shore of the island. Although reefs nearly encircle Cozumel, the windward eastern shore is continuously pounded by heavy wave action, making it dangerous for sport diving. The western side of the island is normally protected from the prevailing tradewinds. With the exception of north-northwest winds that frequently blow during the late fall and sometimes during the early winter, the sea on Cozumel's western side is normally calm.

All divers coming to Cozumel are strongly urged to visit the Museum of the Island of Cozumel where you will find a wealth of information about the reef formations, natural history, Mayan culture and contemporary history. A visit to the museum will make you more aware of the need to practice environmentally sound diving.

SHORE DIVING

There are many areas teeming with interesting marine life that can be easily reached from shore. These sites provide inexpensive dives to supplement the wide assortment of boat dive packages offered on the island.

Except in unusually rough conditions, the shore dives listed here offer easy entries and exits. Access is generally over sandy beaches or down stairways cut into the ironshore. All of the shoreline in Cozumel is open to the public. This includes access to the water in front of hotels. With your C-card, you can rent a tank and then take a taxi with all your equipment to the dive site. You may be able to arrange in advance to have a tank waiting for you, as there are dive operations at many of the entry points listed in this book as shore dive sites.

There is a particularly enjoyable night drift dive along the shore between the new lighthouse and the Scuba Club Cozumel. Take a taxi to the light house and enter the water at the small protected beach. In water less than 20 feet (6 m) you will encounter many octopuses, literally dozens of pufferfishes, sea horses, spotted rays, sharp tailed eels and an endless variety of invertebrates.

Even those hotels that don't have a reef close to shore have excellent shore diving opportunities. Tires and other manmade items placed offshore at the Scuba Club Cozumel offer a great place to look for octopus, eels, trunkfish, hermit crabs and a variety of other nocturnal feeders. This makes an especially good night dive location.

BOAT DIVING

There are a wide variety of dive boats operating in Cozumel. Fifteen to twenty years ago, almost all of the dive boats were the slow "motor-sailers." These boats often took hours to reach the spectacular, southernmost reefs, making a two-tank boat trip into a whole day affair. Today, however, almost all of the dive operations use fast boats, most of which are equipped with heavy-duty twin outboard motors. These boats usually leave the dock between 8:00 and 9:00 A.M. for a two-tank boat trip and return between 11:30 A.M. and 1:00 P.M., depending upon the location of your hotel and distance to the sites. With the faster boats, resorts on the north side of town can also run half-day trips to the south. In peak season and whenever there is sufficient demand, many of the dive resorts will run two-tank trips in the afternoon as well as the morning.

Flamingo tongue cowries can often be found grazing on the stalks of gorgonian sea fans. The decorative spots are actually part of a retractable mantle.

Divers load their gear onto the dive boat for a day of adventure under the sea.

Divers wait to be picked up after a drift dive. Almost all dives on Cozumel are conducted as drift dives because of the current.

Octopusses are a common sight on shallow night dives.

Resorts that book week-long dive packages will try to keep the same group of divers together throughout the course of the week so that everyone will get to experience as many different reefs as possible. It is also standard practice that the less difficult dives are made in the beginning of the week and the more advanced dive sites later in the week. In this way divers are given a chance to become familiar with drift diving and lets the guides determine individual skill levels within the groups.

Of course, there are a large number of independent dive operators with small, fast boats. Most of these operations have boats that hold six to eight divers. They are an excellent choice for small groups because they can cater to the group's specific desires. Groups of experienced divers may want to set up special trips where they can arrange to go only to the more exciting, advanced sites. Other groups may elect to dive reefs which require only intermediate skill levels. Or a group may prefer to return to the same site repeatedly.

CURRENTS AND CORAL

The dominant current flowing through the Caribbean originates in the South Atlantic. When the current reaches the Brazilian bulge it splits. About 40 percent of the flow moves along the north face of South America and into the Caribbean Sea. This flow is called the Guiana Current. Because the earth's rotation causes currents to bend clockwise in the northern hemisphere, the Guiana is flowing almost due north as it sweeps around Cozumel.

This large volume of water is severely constricted as it flows through the narrow Yucatan Channel which spans about 100 miles (161 km) between Mexico and Cuba. This constriction results in the current reaching speeds of over 2 knots in the Channel and as much as 8 knots between Cozumel and the mainland.

Corals thrive in strong current which constantly delivers oxygenated and carbonated water to support their metabolism, and at the same time, sweeps away foul sediments. The most massive coral formations on Cozumel lie off the south shore which faces the current.

The excellent water clarity found in Cozumel enhances the amount of sunlight penetrating the water, thus increasing coral calcification and growth.

Because much of Cozumel is made up of porous materials such as ironshore, rain water rapidly percolates into the ground and travels to the sea through subterranean channels. This lack of surface rivers and runoff prevents fouling of the reefs.

As currents bend around the west side of Cozumel, a small, clockwise eddy sometimes forms. This temporary condition causes a southward current near the shore, usually between San Miguel and Punta Tormentos. A more permanent eddy persists on the northern side of the island. Some of the water which has swept up to the north becomes caught in these spiral circulations and rapidly slows down. Fine sediment and coral debris that was suspended in the formerly fast moving current settles to the bottom, producing a flat, marshy shore with mangroves and large, shallow sand bank.

The northeasterly trade winds, which cool off the afternoons, also create the predominant wave swell out of the northeast. Since Cuba acts as a breakwater, the wave action striking Cozumel is moderate. The sandy bottom on the east coast is stirred up by frequent wave action which smothers significant coral growth. However, tubeworms and coralline algae have constructed a few large, cemented reef formations here. The wave action is also sufficient to create a littoral drift along the shore, which transports sand from the north depositing it along the eastern shore. This flow of sand produces the east coast beaches and the sand bank on the south end of Cozumel which terminates with sand falls dropping off between the giant buttresses of the southern reefs.

DRIFT DIVING

Almost all boat diving in Cozumel is drift diving. The Guiana Current that runs in a northerly direction sweeps up to the southern end of the island, producing currents of variable strength. These currents are almost always present and tend to run from south to north. Currents often change in intensity and even direction during the course of a dive, necessitating experienced dive guides as well as boat captains.

Once the boat reaches the dive site and

divers are geared up, the dive guide will give a short description of the site and outline the dive plan, including depth and time. All divers leave the boat at the same time and meet the guide on the sand bottom next to the reef.

As soon as everyone is ready, the divers move off in the same direction as the current. Most of the time, the currents can be quite strong, sometimes reaching two knots or more. When you get used to drift diving, you will find that this type of diving is almost effortless. You use your buoyancy control to stay off the bottom and just drift along the reef using the current to carry you along. As the divers drift with the current below the surface of the water, the boat follows the group's bubbles.

Most of the dive guides will allow buddy teams to do their own thing as long as they have demonstrated they are competent divers and they adhere to the depth limit set by the guide. When divers reach a designated minimum tank pressure, they ascend to the surface and wait for the boat to pick them up. All divers should do a "drift" safety stop at 15 feet (5 m). It is strongly recommended that a signal device such as a bright orange inflatable safety sausage be carried by each diver.

EQUIPMENT

There are several large dive stores in addition to quite a number of small operations on Cozumel. Good rental gear can be obtained from reputable shops. However, to ensure fit and reliability of diving equipment, divers should have their own mask, regulator, buoyancy compensator and gauges whenever traveling abroad.

MARINE LIFE PRESERVATION

The Cozumel Association of Dive Operators (CADO) has developed a list of basic diving guidelines in order to preserve the marine life.

- On boat dives, all divers descend onto sandy areas adjacent to the reefs, and not directly on top of corals. This allows divers to adjust their buoyancy without damaging any coral.
- Divers should attain neutral buoyancy before swimming over reefs.
- Divemasters and instructors are encouraged to do what they can to get divers to minimize the amount of weight they wear.
- Any gear that might drag along the surface of the reef such as dangling gauges or octopus regulators should be secured.
- Divers should stay at least three feet away from corals, sponges and other delicate animals.
- No marine animals should be collected. Within the National Marine Park, it is against the law to take corals, sponges, shells, or other marine life. All of the dive sites detailed in this book, except for Barracuda, Cantarell and San Juan Reefs, lie within the National Marine Park.

At night, divers will often see basket stars perched atop coral heads, sea fans or whip corals. Basket stars feed at night and hide in the reef during the day.

All reputable operators require divers to hang at 15 feet (5 m) for a three-minute safety stop at the end of every dive.

SAFETY

In recent years, the diving practices in Cozumel have come under a great deal of scrutiny. Operations have been criticized for not adhering to safe diving practices, for accepting unqualified divers, and for taking divers on dives that are well beyond their skill levels.

Over the last 12 years, I have made hundreds of dives on the island and have become familiar with most of the dive operations. Although I have heard several stories about unsafe dive operations, I have personally never experienced any, with the possible exception of marginally short surface intervals between multiple dives.

Since the Cozumel Association of Dive Operations (CADO) was formed in the late 1980's, there has been an even greater emphasis on safety. Divers can expect the following procedures by CADO members:

- When divers check in, they must present their C-cards, and in some cases their log books.
- Operators will often conduct a shallow water checkout dive to evaluate a diver's capabilities and to allow each diver to check his or her gear.
- Divers completing only a resort course will be limited to a maximum depth of 40 feet (12 m).
- The more difficult dives will be done near the end of the vacation so divers have a chance to "work up" to those dives.
- Deep dives are always the first dive of the day and are usually limited to depths of 80 or 90 feet (24 or 27 m). Advanced divers with more experience are permitted to go on some deeper dives in more remote areas.
- Second dives on a two-tank dive trip are made on depths shallower than 60 feet (18 m) after an appropriate surface interval.
- Divers are encouraged to take a minimum three-minute safety stop at 15 feet (5 m) at the end of every dive.
- Most operations provide one divemaster for groups up to ten, and two divemasters for groups of more than ten.

Patience in exploring small crevices will produce many surprises on shallow reefs like this splendid toadfish (Sanopus splendidus).

UNDERWATER TERRAIN

Cozumel is oriented along a north/south axis. A drop-off roughly parallels the western shoreline from Punte Norte at the northwest corner of the island to Punta Celarain at the south end of the island. Most of the reefs are located at the lip of the drop-off at a variety of depths. The reefs can be roughly categorized according to their depths as either shallow, mid-depth or deep reefs, although the bottom contours and reef types vary greatly. The depths and the intensity of the currents dictate whether sites are considered as novice, intermediate or advanced.

There is a tremendous variety of corals in Cozumel. Purple and pink gorgonian fans are found in great numbers in the shallow areas where there is considerable wave action. Brain corals, whip corals and lettuce corals are commonly seen as a patchwork of color on most mid-depth reefs. On deeper reefs and on the wall dives, there are huge tube sponges, tangles of rope sponge, black coral and large deep water gorgonians.

VISIBILITY

The underwater visibility in Cozumel is usually the best that can be found in the entire Caribbean, averaging 150 feet (45 m) year-round and often reaching 200 feet (61 m) or more. This extreme clarity sometimes makes it possible for boat captains to actually see the divers as they swim along the bottom.

WATER TEMPERATURE

The water around Cozumel is warm all year. The temperature varies from a low of 77°F (25°C) in the winter and a high of 84°F (29°C) in the late summer months. While a dive skin is sufficient protection from cuts, scrapes and abrasions during the warmer months, it is a good idea to wear a 1/8 inch (3mm) wet suit for extra warmth from November through March. A hooded vest is another option during the colder months.

COZUMEL
SHORE DIVING
1. North of the International Pier
2. The Amphitheater
3. International Pier
4. Paradise Shallows
5. Cozumel Reef Hotel Reef
6. Chankanaab Underwwater Park
CAVERN AND CAVE DIVING
7. Tres Potrillos (The Three Ponies)
BOAT DIVING
8. The Scuba Club, Villablanca and El Cid-La Ceiba Drop-offs
9. Paradise Reef
10. Las Palmas Drop-off
11. Chankanaab Reef
12. Felipe Xicotencatl (C-53 Wreck)
13. Tormentos Reef
14. Yucab Reef
15. Punta Tunich Drop-off
16. San Francisco Reef
17. Santa Rosa Reef
18. Paso Del Cedral Reef
19. La Francesca Reef
20. Dalila Reef
21. Palancar Shallows
22. Palancar Horseshoe
23. Palancar Caves
24. Columbia Gardens
25. Columbia Pinnacles
26. Punta Sur Reef
27. Maracaibo Reef
LESS FREQUENTED SITES
28. Cantarell Reef
29. Barracuda Reef
30. San Juan Reef
31. Cardona Reef
32. Palancar Deep
33. Chun Chacaab
Point Molas Lighthouse
CARIBBEA

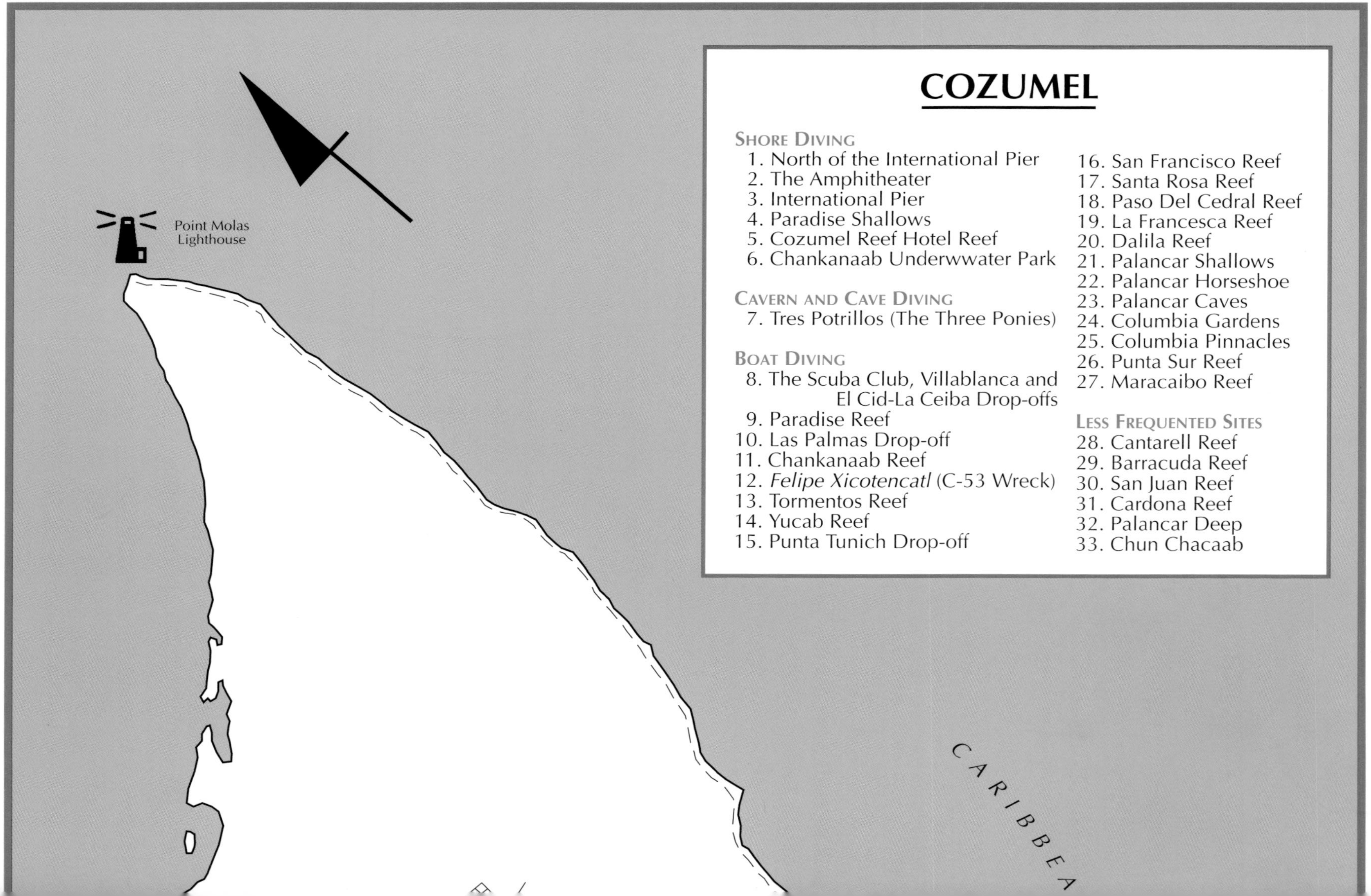

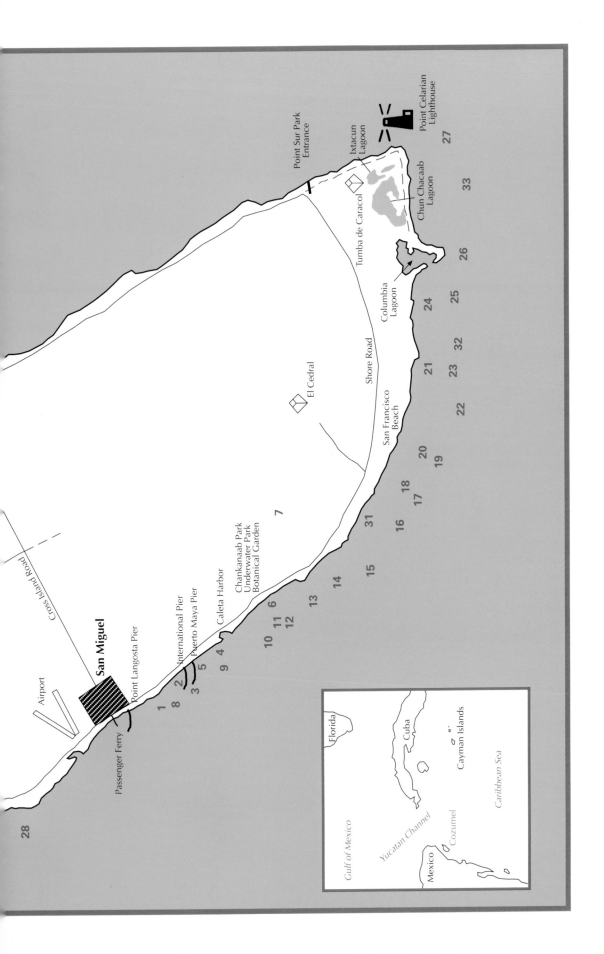

Airport

Cross Island Road

San Miguel

Passenger Ferry

Point Langosta Pier

International Pier

Puerto Maya Pier

Caleta Harbor

Chankanaab Park
Underwater Park
Botanical Garden

El Cedral

Shore Road

San Francisco Beach

Columbia Lagoon

Tumba de Caracol

Point Sur Park Entrance

Ixtacun Lagoon

Chun Chacaab Lagoon

Point Celarian Lighthouse

28

1
8
2
3
5
9
4
10
11
12
6
13
14
15
31
16
17
18
19
20
21
22
23
32
24
25
26
33
27
7

Gulf of Mexico

Florida

Cuba

Cayman Islands

Yucatan Channel

Cozumel

Mexico

Caribbean Sea

CHAPTER **VI** DIVE SITES

SHORE DIVING

1. NORTH OF INTERNATIONAL PIER

DEPTH:	15-25 FEET
	(5-8 M)
CURRENT:	LIGHT

A shallow reef runs roughly parallel to the shoreline, beginning about a mile (1.6 km) south of San Miguel. This reef, which consists of small coral heads, scattered gorgonians and sea whips, lies close to shore.

The first section begins in front of the Lorena Hotel. The second section, divided by a wide open stretch of sand and eel grasses, is laid out in a continuous string of scattered coral heads from the Villablanca Hotel south to the International Pier next to the El Cid-La Ceiba Resort. Most of the coral heads are between 15 and 25 feet (5-8 m) deep. Different sections of this reef can be accessed from the Lorena Hotel, the pier across the street from the Villablanca Hotel, the Del Mar Aquatics pier and the pier at the El Cid-La Ceiba Hotel.

The marine life is interesting and varied. There are a tremendous number of invertebrates including arrow crabs, octopuses, live shells, hermit crabs, fire worms and tube worms. Divers will also discover many spotted rays, trunkfish, small moray eels, pufferfish and even an occasional sea horse. Juvenile angelfishes, spotted drums, and filefishes are common amongst the coral heads.

2. THE AMPHITHEATER

DEPTH:	35 FEET
	(11 M)
CURRENT:	NONE TO
	MODERATE

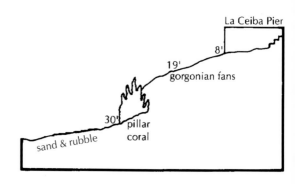

In 1977, a 40-passenger, twin engine DC3 was purposely sunk as a prop for a Mexican disaster film. The owners of the La Ceiba Hotel saved the plane to be used as an artificial reef and dive site just off the hotel. In recent years, the plane wreck has been overturned, damaged and moved during various storms. It now rests in 35 feet of (11m) of water, about 65 yards (60 m) offshore. There is a small buoy that marks the location, straight out from the end of the pier at the north end of the El Cid-La Ceiba Hotel property. The increase in the

Beautiful sponges grow along the vertical wall at the north end of Santa Rosa Reef.

Turtles are abundant on the reefs of Cozumel and are always a welcome sight.

number of cruise ships has significantly affected this site. Their props have covered the wreck with sand, but there is still an abundance of marine life here. Access to the area can be gained through the El Cid-La Ceiba Hotel or the adjacent Del Mar Aquatics pier. If you are staying at another hotel or resort, you can take a taxi to one of these piers. Just throw your dive gear in the trunk. It's a good idea to take a towel along to dry off after the dive and to sit on during the return taxi ride. You can walk through the lobby of the hotel to get to the walkway along the water's edge. There are two main access points to the water along this walkway: one set of stairs near the hotel pool and the other next to the pier. Another access point is located at the Del Mar Aquatics pier just to the north of the El Cid-La Ceiba Hotel.

There is rarely much wave chop or heavy current here because the area sits in a protected "V" between the shoreline and the International Pier. During the day the site is visited by large schools of grunts, snapper and a variety of reef fishes. An assortment of anemones, small shrimp and arrow crabs can be found clinging to coral and bits of rubble.

The flat sandy area abuts against a steep slope on the shore side. Here, the bottom rises quickly to between 15 and 20 feet (5-6 m) and then levels off. From the top edge of this slope, the bottom rises gradually to the shoreline. There are many purple gorgonian fans scattered around the coral heads in this shallow area. Flamingo tongue cowries, with their striking spotted mantles, can be found on most of these fans. Divers will also find hundreds of Christmas tree tube worms protruding from the corals, as well as hermit crabs, mantis shrimp, and tiny blennies. As an added treat, divers have found sea horses in this area. All of these tiny animals offer excellent subjects for macro photography.

The area along the steep slope is crowded with large coral heads, including some impressive pinnacles of pillar coral. This shallow reef consisting of numerous coral heads extends to the north and south along the shore. Look closely for cleaning stations with juvenile Spanish hogfish.

Excellent night dive. The shallows offer an excellent night dive location. When you enter the water, get your bearings on the set of lights that are located near your exit point.

The scattered coral heads around the plane are teeming with life at night. The schools of grunts that are present during the day, disperse over the sandy bottom to forage for food. Spiny lobsters and slipper lobsters are very common in this area, as are octopuses, eels and toadfish. For the serious photographers and videographers, this area is superb at night. There is little or no current, and with the shallow depth, bottom time is almost unlimited.

3. INTERNATIONAL PIER

DEPTH:	20-30 FEET
	(6-9 M)
CURRENT:	LIGHT TO
	MODERATE

As with most piers, the pilings have a great deal of growth, and the bottom around the pilings is littered with rubble and assorted man-made materials.

The rubble on the bottom comes to life at night, making this an interesting place for close-up and macro photography, and video. The pilings and rubble are covered with colorful encrusting sponges and corals. Look for orange ball anemones, hermit crabs, splendid toadfish, yellow stingrays, rough file clams, balloonfish, moray eels and a variety of other interesting marine life. In the water column around the piling, divers will often find schools of small jacks, barracuda and squid.

Caution. Because of the comings and goings of large cruise ships and other ferry boats, this area can be dangerous. Unfortunately, there are so many cruise ships visiting Cozumel on a daily basis, it is a rarity that the pier is unused. Also, the car ferry makes frequent trips between this pier and ports on the mainland. There is considerable danger from the huge

props on these ships, which cause strong suction and turbulence. If you really want to dive this area you should check with the harbor master to obtain a schedule of times when the area will be free of ships arriving or leaving from the pier.

4. PARADISE SHALLOWS

DEPTH:	20 FEET
	(6 M)
CURRENT:	LIGHT

Paradise Shallows, also known as Caleta Reef, is a continuation of the patch reef that runs from the Lorena Hotel to the International Pier. This site consists of widely scattered coral heads, sponges and other corals, such as sea whips and sea fans. It continues south, paralleling the shoreline, from the International Pier to Caleta Lagoon. Paradise Shallows is situated between the shore and Paradise (Paraiso) Reef. Depth averages 20 feet (6 m).

When the current is running from south to north, as it usually does, it is possible to swim out to Paradise Shallows from shore. There are lots of exit points as you drift toward the north, including the International Pier and several hotel piers just beyond. When making a shore dive, it is a good idea to take a small waterproof container with sufficient money for the return taxi ride and perhaps some refreshments at the end of the dive.

5. COZUMEL REEF HOTEL REEF

DEPTH:	20 FEET
	(6 M)
CURRENT:	LIGHT

This shallow site is close to shore and accessible from the Beach Club Located across the street from the Cozumel Reef Hotel (Holiday Inn). Although this area suffered extreme damages from the 1988 hurricane, there is a dramatic amount of new coral and sponge growth on the gently sloping bottom. A variety of reef fishes and other marine life can

Chankanaab Park offers swimming, snorkeling and scuba as well as a dolphin workshop, sea lion show and botanical garden.

be seen here. There is a mixture of hardpan, sand and rubble bottom, which supports a variety of sponges and corals, including corky sea fingers and gorgonians. Look for spotted trunkfishes, trumpetfishes, filefishes and angelfishes.

6. CHANKANAAB UNDERWATER PARK

DEPTH:	15-35 FEET
	(5-11M)
CURRENT:	NONE TO LIGHT

The Chankanaab Underwater Park is probably the most popular and well known shore dive on Cozumel. The name means "little ocean" and comes from the picturesque lagoon at the Park. The lagoon, now only a few feet deep, used to be connected to the ocean by a short tunnel through which divers could swim. That tunnel is now closed off, and the lagoon is off limits to everyone. There are a couple of

A large school of friendly snapper hang out on a coral head just offshore from the access steps at Chankanaab Park.

wooden observation platforms next to the lagoon for fish watching in this outdoor, natural aquarium. On the northern edge of the Park, there is a shallow, protected sandy cove where swimming is permitted. The cove is located just south of the dolphin pens. Also located at the Park are several gift stores and boutiques, white sand beaches, a botanical garden, a sea lion show, dolphin encounters, and a museum which explains the history of Chankanaab. In additon, there is a dive store, restaurant and fresh water showers. Chankanaab is an excellent place to spend a whole day diving, snorkeling, sunning, eating, and taking a stroll on the shaded pathways.

The Park police seriously enforce the restrictions against the use of knives or wearing gloves inside the Park's waters. On the oceanside of the Park, there are steps and railings for assistance getting in and out of the water. The coral and rocky surfaces in the shallows are covered with multi-colored Christmas tree tube worms. There are several high profile coral heads about 25 yards (23 m) offshore. At one particularly large coral head directly offshore from the steps at the main part of the Park, schools of friendly snapper and grunts can usually be found in only 20 to 30 feet (6-9 m) of water. This is an excellent place to snorkel or have an orientation dive.

CAVERN AND CAVE DIVING

The cave and cenote systems of the Yucatan Peninsula are world famous for their spectacular formations and amazing clarity of water. Cozumel offers three separate cave systems and each one is uniquely beautiful. Divers must be cave certified to access the cave systems on their own or they may be allowed to do a cavern dive or cave intro dive with a NACD or NSSCDS instructor, specially equipped with appropriate gear.

Cavern dives are always within the daylight zone. The maximum penetration is 200 feet (61 m) at a depth of 60 feet (18 m) with excellent visibility. The water in these underground rivers is very clear. Requirements for cavern diving is an open water certificate, a certified guide and a desire for adventure.

Cave dives are deeper penetrations into extensive cave systems or cenote dives (no ambient light and complete overhead obstruction), both of which require special training and special safety equipment. The water temperature in the cenotes on Cozumel averages 79°F (26°C) and visibility averages around 100 feet (30 m). There are also visible haloclines, where the layers of fresh and salt water meet.

Ramon Zapata Caves (Chankanaab Cave System). The National Parks are now working on a new cave diving program, offering access to the Ramon Zapata Caves on the south end of the park facility at Chankanaab. For certified cave divers with appropriate equipment, and advanced divers accompanied by Park approved dive guides, there are two sets of caves which actually penetrate back under the shoreline. Most of the diving depths are shallow, no more than 20 feet (6 m). The cave entrance is only 10 feet (3 m) deep and is located about 75 yards (68 m) to the south of the main Park. There are several wide openings to a large cavern that has tunnels heading off in many different directions. This system of caves has been explored by expert cave divers for a distance of over 1,650 yards (1,500 m) into the interior of the island.

Caution. Cave diving requires special training and equipment. Do not leave the cavern (natural light) zone unless you are a certified cave diver with the proper cave diving equipment.

To find the entrance to the caves, follow the shore line closely to the south until you see a large cut or channel. The caves are located on the Park side of this cut. In the outer cavern, it is common to find large tarpon and swarms of small, silvery baitfish floating through large underwater chambers. Some people refer to this area as **Beachcomber Cavern**, reputedly named after a restaurant that used to sit beside the cut when the old road passed directly along the shoreline. The road has since been moved inland so that is doesn't interfere with the ecology or detract from the esthetics of the Park. Divers have discovered Mayan Pottery in the interior of the cave.

Aerolito de Paraiso is another extensive underwater cave system on Cozumel offering two entrances with easy access. There are many stalactites and stalagmites only 50 yards (46 m) from the entrance. The most interesting areas are the Wonderland Room and the Bozanic Passage. The maximum depth is 60 feet (18 m) with an estimated 1,200-foot (364 m) penetration.

Large silvery tarpon cruise about the recesses of the caves at Chankanaab.

7. TRES POTRILLOS (THE THREE PONIES)

DEPTH:	125 FEET
	(38 M)
LEVEL:	CAVE DIVE

The entrance to Los Tres Potrillos (The Three Ponies) cave is a 3-foot by 3-foot (1x1 m) hole in the ground.

Aerolito de Paraiso is an extensive underwater cave system offering two entrances with easy access. There are many stalactites and stalagmites in this system.

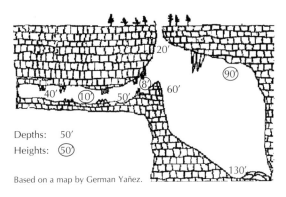

Depths: 50'
Heights: 50

Based on a map by German Yañez.

Los Tres Potrillos is a sinkhole recently discovered by German Yañez Mendoza. German is a certified NACD and NSSCDS cave dive instructor and the owner of Yucatech Expeditions on Cozumel. The entrance to this remarkable cave is located in the middle of the jungle, a short distance from the new highway that runs along the west coast of Cozumel. Diving is restricted to certified cave divers or advanced divers accompanied by a certified cave diving guide. Anyone interested in experiencing this dive should contact Yucatech Expeditions and arrange for a tour.

The entrance to the cenote is a 3- by 3-foot (1 x 1m) hole in the ground located on a ranch south of San Miguel. The dive requires special equipment including double tanks, backup lights and hand lines. Accessing the dive requires a 10-minute trek in full gear down a partially overgrown foot path. The small hole in the ground is covered by an iron grate. To enter the dive, you ease yourself fins first, into the coffee colored water and drop straight down for about 20 feet (6 m). The discoloration is caused by tannins from the surrounding foliage. At a depth of about 25 feet (8 m), the hole suddenly widens into a huge cavern and the water clarity increases to nearly 100 feet (30 m). A guide line has been affixed to the sides of the cavern. Off to one side of the cavern there is a long cave at a depth of 50 to 60 feet (15-18 m), that penetrates approximately 50 yards (46 m) horizontally. This cave is filled with delicate stalactites—both soda straws and columns—and stalagmites. The walls are embedded with fossils, including whale bones and shells of all shapes and sizes. There are also incredible and mysterious formations throughout. The bottom of the cavern drops to 130 feet (39 m) at its deepest corner. This dive is not for the faint at heart. It combines a marathon walk, a claustrophobic entry, no penetration of natural light, overhead obstruction, and excessive depths. Despite these minor difficulties, the dive is an awesome experience.

BOAT DIVING

8. THE SCUBA CLUB, VILLABLANCA AND EL CID-LA CEIBA DROP-OFFS

DEPTH:	30-130+ FEET
	(9-39+ M)
CURRENT:	MODERATE TO
	STRONG

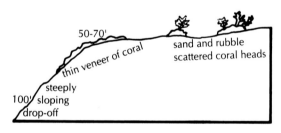

These three sites are actually contiguous sections of the continuous wall that runs along the entire west coast of Cozumel 200 to 400 yards (182-364 m) offshore. The terrain and resident fishes are very similar throughout this area. A mostly sandy bottom, dotted with small coral heads, gorgonian fans and large sponges, slopes gently from the shore to the edge of the drop-offs which begin at depths between 50 and 70 feet (15-21 m). While the wall is fairly steep in most places, some areas are nearly vertically. Large green morays eels can frequently be found cruising the reef during the day. The lip of the wall from the Scuba Club Cozumel Resort to the El Cid-La Ceiba Hotel

runs roughly parallel to shore and is several hundred yards (meters) off the beach. The back reef on the shore side averages a depth of 35 feet (11 m) and is relatively flat. Here, divers will find sharp tailed eels, nurse sharks, schools of cottonwicks, and a tremendous variety of invertebrates. This area is also a nursery for an incredible mix of tropical fishes, including angelfishes, filefishes and puffers.

These sites are rarely visited because of their close proximity to many of the major hotels. In addition, there is not very much coral buildup on the lip of the drop-off as there is at some of the more popular reefs further to the south.

Because the currents are frequently strong in this area, there is a good chance to see schools of baitfish, bar jacks, horse-eye jacks and larger pelagics, such as barracuda, grouper and an occasional ray or shark. These sites are not recommended as shore dives because of the distances from shore, the depths, and the potential for very strong currents.

9. PARADISE REEF

DEPTH:	22-40 FEET
	(7-12 M)
CURRENT:	LIGHT TO
	MODERATE

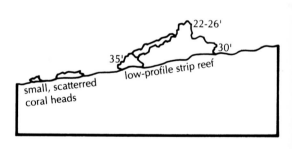

Paradise (Paraiso) Reef consists of four separate ridges, lined up roughly end to end and running parallel to shore. The reef begins about 150 to 200 yards (136-182 m) straight out from the entrance to the Celeta Lagoon located on the north side of the Presidente Inter-Continental Hotel. It continues on toward the International Pier. The ridges rise only 5 to 10 feet (2-3 m) above a flat sandy bottom and are 25-40 yards (23-36 m) wide in most places. There are a few solitary pinnacles in

The lip of the drop-off at the Scuba Club Cozumel wall is dotted with red sponges, deep-water gorgonian fans and many large barrel sponges.

The La Ceiba Drop-off has a large number of huge, brown tub and barrel sponges.

Splendid toadfish, one of the unique varieties of marine life in Cozumel are usually seen peering out from under ledges.

the center of the reef. The maximum depth here is 40 feet (12 m). The currents at Paradise Reef are light to moderate, and usually run south to north toward the International Pier. While there are few caves and tunnels within the reef structures, there are a myriad of cracks, crevices and overhangs on either side of the reef. The terrain is not spectacular, but the marine life is varied and abundant.

Keep in mind, when diving this area, that the reef sections are not lined up exactly end to end. There is a wide sand channel between the largest sections of the reef, and in one area you must swim diagonally to your left to find the beginning of the next section of the reef. Check out the eel grass and rubble bottom at the end of the second section of the reef on the shore side. Here you will often find sea horses up to six inches (15 cm) long.

Splendid toadfish. Paradise Reef is one of the best places to find Cozumel's toadfish, which goes by the common names of "Cozumel catfish" or "splendid toadfish." This unusual animal can usually be found peeking out from low ledges on the sand bottom on either side of the reef. The toadfish has a wide, compressed head with whisker-like appendages extending from the underside of its mouth. It has horizontal white and charcoal blue, gray stripes on its head and body, with all of its fins lined in bright yellow.

Small schools of grunt and snapper can be found tucked into the cuts and crevices in the reef, or grouped around the prevalent whip corals. Feeding stations with juvenile hogfish and cleaner wrasse can be found everywhere. Orange filefish, cowfish, scrawled filefish, grouper and various types of parrotfishes are among the most common fishes on the reef. It is also a good place to see spotted moray eels, which will often swim out of the reef during the day. Don't extend your fingers in front of the eels. The combination of a good appetite and poor eyesight can lead them to mistake your fingers for a handout.

The reef has lots of small vase sponges and a wonderful variety of anemones. For macro photography, there are many small animals including hermit crabs, banded shrimp, arrow crabs, Christmas tree tube worms and bristle worms.

Because of its location and depth, this site is usually visited as a shallow second dive after a deeper wall dive.

Popular night dive. Paradise is the most popular site for boat night diving. Divers will almost always be treated to appearances by octopuses, toadfish, eels, puffers, trunkfish and a variety of sleeping reef fishes.

10. LAS PALMAS DROP-OFF

DEPTH:	50-100+ FEET
	(15-30+ M)
CURRENT:	MODERATE TO
	STRONG

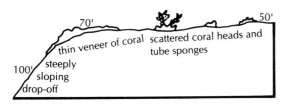

The Las Palmas drop-off is named after the tall, lonely looking palm tree which stands by itself just on the north side of the Fiesta Americana Cozumel Hotel. The sand and rubble bottom slopes gently downward to the top of the drop-off in approximately 70 feet (21 m) of water. The currents usually run from south to north along this reef and are often quite strong.

The lip of the drop-off is dotted with large deep-water gorgonian fans, enormous basket sponges and large coral heads. At this site, it is often fairly easy to video and to photograph some of the more skittish varieties of fish such as queen angels. This is because there aren't many caves and crevices for them to dart into, and they seem reluctant to leave the shelter of their adopted coral head. Above the reef, in the water column, divers will frequently see schools of silvery baitfish and rainbow runners,

often pursued by large jacks or barracuda.

The wall itself is very steep in most places. Pairs of large angelfishes, shy squirrelfishes, and small reef fishes are common. The deeper you go, the greater are the chances you will see large pelagics. Small black tip reef sharks make an occasional appearance.

11. CHANKANAAB REEF

DEPTH:	35-50 FEET
	(11-17 M)
CURRENT:	MODERATE

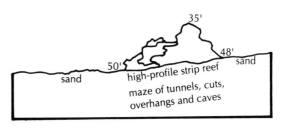

Chankanaab Reef lies several hundred yards (meters) offshore just south of the Park at Chankanaab Lagoon. The reef has two distinct sections separated by a wide sand and rubble channel.

North Section

The northern section is a high profile strip reef with many cuts, tunnels, overhangs and caves. This section sits on a fairly flat sand and rubble bottom with an average depth of 50 feet (15 m). The ridge rises to within 35 feet (11 m) of the surface.

Huge lobsters. The northern area has lots of huge, spiny lobsters (two varieties), some weighing over 20 pounds (9 kg). This is also an excellent area to observe juvenile hogfish pick parasites from various reef fish that wait patiently in line to be cleaned. Black grouper are also fairly common here. In addition, there are lots of bright yellow, red, orange, and fluorescent purple sponges.

The ridge section is honey combed with a maze of tunnels and caves that teem with marine life. Divers will encounter lobsters and crabs as well as an assortment of bigeye and glasseye squirrelfish, large porgies, and small

A banded shrimp forages for food on the branches of a deep-water gorgonian.

BLACK CORAL

Black coral is a member of the gorgonian family, and is usually found only in areas where there is little light and strong currents. Black coral reproduces itself by a larva, which is negatively phototoxic, so it seeks out dark areas to grow. In shallower depths, black coral is found in caves and caverns. It is also found in the open on deep vertical walls, where little light penetrates. When viewed underwater with a dive light, branches of black coral appear orange-brown to orange-red.

Among the characteristics that add value to the black coral are the veins in the center of the stalks which represent different stages of growth. Accumulations of calcium are accentuated with brownish and reddish tones.

schools of margates and grunts.

South Section

The second section, at the south end, consists of a patch reef made up of broad sections of ridges, ending in a scattering of large coral heads. This section is a bit shallower than the north end, with the bottom ranging between 40 and 45 feet (12-14 m).

Good night dive. This is a popular night boat dive location. At night you will find the lobsters out on top of the reef. There is also an abundance of toadfish, eels, puffers, octopuses and sleeping fishes. One unusual sight to look for is a sleeping parrotfish which has enveloped itself in a protective cocoon.

Pairs of gray angelfish are among the most common of the reef fishes found in the clear waters around the island.

12. *FELIPE XICOTENCATL* (C-53 WRECK)

DEPTH:	82 FEET
	(25 M)
CURRENT:	MODERATE TO
	STRONG
TYPE:	MINESWEEPER

Like all shipwrecks, the Felipe Xicotencatl, *lends an aura of mystery to the explorers.*

The *Flipe Zicotencatl* lies on a flat sand bottom, offshore from Chankanaab National Park, northwest of Tormentos Reef. The wreck sits upright in 82 feet (25 m) of water and is parallel to the shoreline with the bow pointing due south. The ship was built in Tampa, Florida in 1942 as a minesweeper for the U.S. Navy. In 1962, the ship was sold to Mexico and was sunk to create an artificial reef in June of 2000. The wreck is 184 feet (56 m) in length and 33 feet (10 m) wide.

The interior of the wreck has been stripped of most obstructions, including machinery, hatches, wiring and sharp objects. There are

three main levels to the wreck not counting the wheelhouse. The lowest level originally contained both engine rooms, crew quarters and a storage room. The second level has several empty rooms on the port and starboard sides, off an interior hallway. This level originally served as the galley, crew showers, offices, officer's cabin and radio room. The third level is the main deck.

A large buoy marks the dive site and there are also floats attached to lines near the bow and stern of the ship. A guideline has been laid out in the interior of the wreck. Escorted dives are usually done with small groups of 4 to 6 divers and usually follow a route indicated by the guide rope. Most areas of the wreck have quite a bit of ambient light, but a handheld dive light is recommended because several areas can be quite dark.

Take a peek under the keel of the wreck. There are usually dozens of large spiny lobster lined up on the sand bottom. The twin propellers are still attached to the main shafts and make excellent photo opportunities. Tours usually begin by entering the wreck on the lowest level through a 4 x 4-foot (1.2 x 1.2 m) cutout near the stern on the port side. Many of the rooms are filled with swarms of baitfish and glassy sweepers. The main deck is at a depth of about 50 feet (15 m), the wheelhouse is at 40 feet (12 m) and the top of the wreck reaches upward to about 30 feet (9 m).

The current in this area can be very strong. When you exit the ship you should take a swim around the exterior to get a feel for the wreck. It is a good idea to stay close to the wreck once you are outside, to avoid being swept away. It is suggested that divers descend and ascend using either the bowline or the stern line. Always begin your ascent with at least 800 psi (55 bars) to allow plenty of air for a safety stop.

The interior of the C-53, a former minesweeper, can be safely penetrated in numerous locations.

13. TORMENTOS REEF

DEPTH:	30-70 FEET
	(9-21 M)
CURRENT:	LIGHT TO
	STRONG

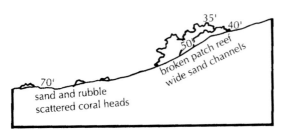

Tormentos Reef is a broken patch reef that protrudes from a sloping, sandy bottom. The reef is located directly out from Punta Tormentos and slightly to the south of Chankanaab Reef. It is named after Punta Tormentos, although sometimes you would swear the reef was named because of the torrential current which frequently scours the area.

There is a sand bar at a depth of 40 feet (12 m) in the middle of the reef. There is a large area on the shore side of the sand bar covered with eel grass. Large 7- to 8-inch (18-21 cm) sea horses are becoming a common attraction in this area.

The south end of the reef begins about 50 yards (46 m) to the north of the end of Yocab Reef across a barren, sandy gap. At this end, the slope begins on a flat sand and rubble bottom in about 30 feet (9 m) of water and drops quickly to a depth of about 60 feet (18 m). It then gradually levels off at 70 feet (21 m) as you get farther from the reef heading toward the drop-off.

Most of the exposed reef structure is between 30 and 60 feet (9-18 m) deep, from the tops of the coral heads to the base of the reef sections. The reef angles toward the northwest so that the north end of the reef reaches a depth of about 70 feet (21 m), and is closer to the drop-off than the southern end.

The majority of the individual sections of the reef extend out across the downward slope making them much higher off the bottom on the offshore side. There are approximately 50 to 70 individual sections of this reef scattered across the sandy bottom. The top of the reef is as shallow as 30 feet (9 m) in some areas, so it usually makes a good site for the second dive of the day.

The reef is decorated with whip corals, brain corals, and a wide variety of colorful sponges. When the current is light, you can get excellent photographs along the top of the reef where there are many small invertebrates, such as flamingo tongue cowries, arrow crabs, banded shrimp, coral shrimp, delicate brittle stars and crinoids. Work with the dive guides to find good locations for pictures. Then set up a shot and wait for your subjects to cruise through the scene.

When the current is strong, it is a good place

Many fishes, such as this stoplight parrotfish, can be approached easily at night.

to drift along taking wide-angle video of groupers and solitary barracuda which hang out in the current. Chubs and yellowtail snapper will usually cluster around visiting divers. Schools of creole wrasse are also common. This is a good area for getting stills or video of swarms of fish hanging around divers.

The north end of the reef is deeper and very lush. Bright orange elephant ear sponges can be found everywhere, making a beautiful back drop for pairs of huge gray angelfish.

As with a number of Cozumel reefs in this depth range, a good place to look for tight schools of margates, snapper, and grunts is beneath overhangs, especially on the down current side of the reef sections. Also look for large angelfishes, and green and spotted moray eels.

14. YUCAB REEF

DEPTH:	35-60 FEET
	(11-18 M)
CURRENT:	MEDIUM TO
	STRONG

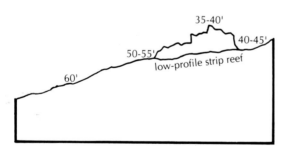

Yucab, occasionally spelled Yocab, is a strip reef that is fairly close to shore, approximately 1ˇ miles (2 km) south of Punta Tormentos (Point Tormentos), just north of Cardona Point. The reef itself is approximately 450 yards (409 m) long and sits on a sand bottom approximately 45 feet (14 m) deep on the shore side and 50 to 55 feet (15-17 m) deep on the offshore side. It is mostly a low-profile reef, rising an average of 8 to 12 feet (2-4 m) off the bottom making diving depths fairly shallow. The top of the reef averages 35-40 feet (11-12 m).

There is usually a medium to strong current moving south to north. Frequent sand channels run perpendicular through the reef, separating it into long sections. Large protected areas where fishes congregate can be found on the down current (north) end of these separate sections.

The resident fishes most often include small schools of silver margates, gray angelfish, French and blue-striped grunts, trunkfishes and porgies, as well as the usually illusive queen angelfish. Divers will also see several types of large black groupers cruising slowly against the current.

The reef ends abruptly as the bottom begins a gradual downward slope. If you continue on a straight line, you would eventually come to the top of the wall at Las Palmas. If you angle off to the left, you will run into the north end of Tormentos Reef. Dive guides will sometimes drop a group in this area and then dive one reef or the other depending on the direction of the current.

Photo tip. Photographers should investigate cuts and overhangs where they will find excellent opportunities to get close-up fish portraits. The fishes seem more intent on staying out of the current than in shying away from divers. As on most shallow reefs in Cozumel, pairs of large, white-spotted orange filefish and scrawled filefish are common. When taking pictures or shooting video of these fishes, keep in mind that they are "almost" always found in pairs. The male will usually try to draw you away from the smaller female. Watch where the female goes and place yourself between the two. The male will usually swim right by you to rejoin its mate.

This cluster of tube worms was found near the base of a coral head facing into the current. These animals have sensors which will usually cause them to retract instantly because of changes in pressure waves, or light in the water.

15. PUNTA TUNICH DROP-OFF

DEPTH:	50-13+ FEET (15-39+ M)
CURRENT:	MODERATE TO STRONG

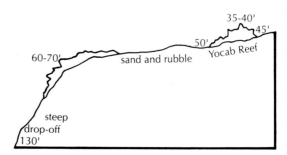

Punta Tunich (Rocky Point), or the Virgin Wall, is a wall dive located directly out from Punta Tunich and several hundred yards outside and parallel to Yucab Reef. The reef begins before the drop-off and continues over the edge. The top of the reef varies between 50 and 80 feet (15-24 m). At the north end of the reef, there is little buildup of coral. The south end of the site is fairly barren with a steeply sloping drop-off. Divers will find lots of squirrelfishes tucked into crevices. Pairs of angelfishes are quite common and are often found heading directly into the face of the current. Aggressive pairs of gray and French angelfish will move amongst the divers.

Vertical drop-off. The north end of this reef has by far the most interesting terrain. The wall becomes more of a vertical drop-off, and is etched with depressions, cuts, tunnels, and caves down to 130 feet (39 m). Here you will see large sponges, deep water fans and even large branches of black coral.

The wall at Punta Tunich has several large green, resident moray eels. The antics between the guides and eels offer unique photo and video opportunities. Guides will often hold and caress the eels.

Caution: Unpredictable current. This site usually experiences strong currents which whisk you along. These currents are unpredictable, not only changing direction from north to south, but also into down currents.

Pairs of large French angelfish will often approach divers along the drop-off at Punta Tunich. The current can become quite strong in this area, allowing divers to drift right up to fishes swimming against the current.

The drop-off along the west coast of Cozumel are ornately adorned with a fascinating variety of sponges.

Schools of porkfish are sometimes found under an expansive ledge and in the caves at Paso Del Cedral.

16. SAN FRANCISCO REEF

DEPTH:	40-100+ FEET
	(12-30+ M)
CURRENT:	MODERATE TO
	STRONG

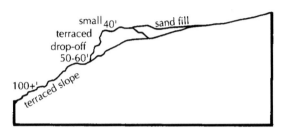

San Francisco Reef is a popular strip reef located approximately a kilometer offshore from San Francisco Beach. The reef sits at the edge of a small drop-off and runs roughly parallel to shore for about 450 yards (409 m). The depths here are between 50 and 60 feet (15-18 m). In some places the top of the reef rises to within 40 feet (12 m) of the surface.

The top of the reef is sand and rubble, with a sloping drop-off. Most of the coral is at, or over, the edge of the lip. The reef is terraced, with a deep drop-off at the north end. Currents here can sometimes be very strong.

There is a good variety of reef fishes, including the ever present pairs of French and gray angels, queen angels, orange and spotted filefish, porgies, jacks, and lots of parrotfishes.

The few tunnels and cuts beneath the reef are quite extensive and definitely worth exploring. Lobsters in the 10- to 15-pound range are frequently seen in deep holes on the sandy bottom.

On the top of the wall, look for fields of tube worms. Hermit crabs are also very abundant. Southern sting rays are often seen feeding in the sandy area on the inside of the reef. On the lip of the drop-off, you will find numerous cleaning stations with tiny cleaner wrasse and juvenile hogfish removing parasites from surgeonfishes, small grouper, and a variety of other fishes.

Photo tip. Photographers will find that squirrelfishes are easier to photograph here than in most areas. Approach them slowly so they are less likely to dart into their holes.

The wall outside of San Francisco Reef is referred to as San Francisco Wall. The drop-off is terraced between 60 and 100 feet (18-30 m). There is little coral structure buildup on these terraces, so only the inside reef is dived, and this site is always used as the second dive on a two-tank trip.

Many ceilings of tunnels and caves are covered with brightly colored rope sponges.

In recent years seahorses have become a common attraction on many of the reefs. Here, a seahorse finds refuge on the lip of the drop-off at Las Palmas.

A diver takes a close look at a seahorse clinging to a bit of eel grass near Paradise Reef.

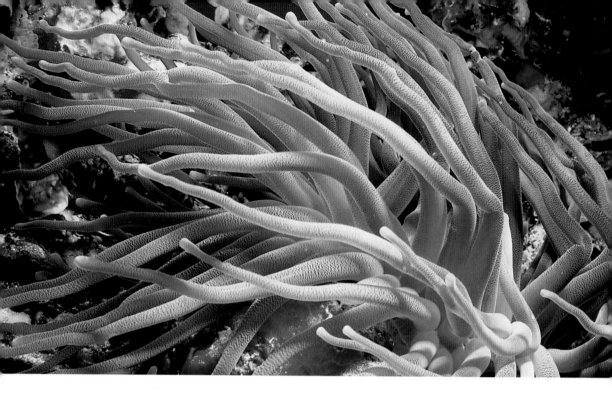

Large anemones are a frequent sight on the deep walls of Santa Rosa.

17. SANTA ROSA REEF

DEPTH:	30-130+ FEET (9-39+ M)
CURRENT:	MODERATE TO STRONG

This interesting area can be divided into three very distinct parts by the appearance of the reef, the configuration of the drop-off, and the predominance of certain varieties of fishes and invertebrates. Unless the current is really strong and you swim with it throughout the dive, it is impossible to see all of Santa Rosa Reef on one tank of air.

The current along the entire length of Santa Rosa is usually moderate to brisk and normally runs south to north. It is often enjoyable to swim a little out from the edge of the reef, and cruise slowly (sometimes fly) along watching the reef, and checking the blue water for something big to come by.

Caution: unpredictable current. At times the current can be strong and unpredictable. You can generally just drop behind an overhang or into a cut or cave to get out of the current. Once in a while, however, there can be a down current which runs up over the top of the reef and straight down the wall. When this occurs, it is advisable to stay on the shoreward side of the reef, which is well-protected.

South Section

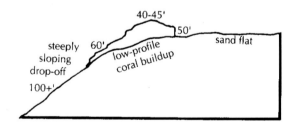

The southernmost part of Santa Rosa has a steeply sloping solid wall that continues into very deep water. As with the entire section of reef, there is a flat sandy area on the shore side where divers are always dropped to begin the dive. This area is approximately 50 feet (15 m) deep at the south end of the reef where the sandy bottom abuts against the inside of the reef. The reef formation itself is built up on the lip of the drop-off, and is mostly an unbroken ridge which rises to about 45 feet (14 m).

The majority of fishes you will see in this area are large angels, a variety of squirrelfishes and the usual assortment of small tropicals. Looking out toward blue water, you will usually see a large number of ocean triggerfish, and an occasional small school of pelagics such as African pompano, crevalle jacks, horse-eye jacks, rainbow runners and bar jacks. Solitary barracuda up to three feet (1 m) in length are also fairly common. In past years, divers occasionally saw one or two blacktip or lemon sharks along this wall at depths below 80 feet (24 m). However, shark sightings at Santa Rosa are becoming rare because of the increasing number of divers.

Middle Section

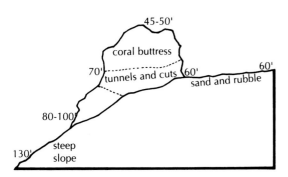

The sand bottom on the shore side of the reef is about 60 feet (18 m) deep and the terrain here begins to take on a much more interesting appearance. The strip reef at the lip of the drop-off is broken into sections. Although the wall itself is still fairly steeply sloped and solid, there are lots of swim-throughs (tunnels and cuts that are big enough to swim through easily), caves and overhangs in the coral. Most of these areas have sandy floors, but on the ceilings of tunnels, you will find an interweaving of brightly colored rope sponges, orange encrusting sponges, and brown tube and barrel sponges. This site is in the 50- to 80-foot (15-24 m) depth range.

Here, divers will encounter large black grouper, barracuda, spotted morays and large green morays. The eels in this area are obviously used to being fed by the guides because they will come out and greet divers, or swim freely inside the tunnels during the day. Spotted eels will also often be found curled up on the sandy floors of some of the tunnels, protruding from the coral walls, or

twisting their way around the surfaces of the reef.

Cowfish and barracuda are commonly seen inside or around the mouths of tunnels and cuts at the top of the drop-off. Approach barracuda slowly. If you see them change from silver to dark with obvious vertical lines, it usually indicates that they are getting agitated or that they are hunting. Although barracuda are generally not dangerous, don't corner them and do not get too close when they display such markings.

This is also a particularly good area to photograph or shoot video of queen angelfish, which will often be seen in groupings of as many as six fish of varying sizes.

There is a long area in this middle section where the reef structure is not built up at the lip of the drop-off. The top of the steeply sloping wall is approximately 60 feet (18 m) deep in this area.

North Section

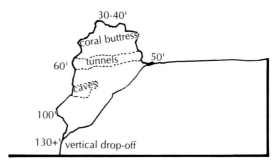

Here, the top of the reef remains broken, but the drop-off becomes more vertical. You can swim through tunnels from the inshore side and end up looking straight down with nothing but dark blue below you. The top of the wall rises to between 30 and 40 feet (9-12 m) in this area. The flat sandy area on the inside of the reef is approximately 50 feet (15 m) deep.

The fish life on top of the reef at this end of Santa Rosa changes quite drastically. There are usually large schools of creole wrasse and many varieties of parrotfishes. There are lots of cleaning stations, as well as interesting invertebrates, such as purple sponges, whip corals, sea rods and corky sea fingers.

There is a noticeable change in the reef structure as you get to the end of the northern section of Santa Rosa. A number of wide sandy channels cut between sections of the reef. The reef ridge turns into a patch reef, with the separate coral heads becoming progressively less massive. Watch for schools of fish in the top of the water column as you decompress at 15 feet (5 m). Schools of bar jacks, creole wrasse and baitfish are quite common.

18. PASO DEL CEDRAL REEF

DEPTH: 35-60 FEET

                (11-18 M)

CURRENT: MODERATE TO

                STRONG

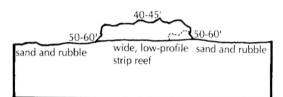

Paso Del Cedral is a patch and strip reef, about 250 yards (227 m) in length, which is frequently broken by perpendicular channels. It is located at the north end of Dalila (at Point Cedral) and to the east (or shore side) of the south end of Santa Rosa Reef. This wide reef sits on a relatively flat sand and rubble bottom in 55 to 60 feet (17-18 m) of water. The current, which fluctuates from moderate to strong, almost always runs in a south to north direction. The top of the reef varies between 35 and 50 feet (11-15 m), and gradually slopes upward at the north end.

Schooling fishes. Paso Del Cedral is one of the best reefs to obtain good photographs of schooling fishes. Many different types of fish school here and the fishes are not too skittish. Inside the various sections of the reef, there is a maze of tunnels, caves and overhangs, where schools of grunts, snapper and margates can be found. Trunkfishes are commonly seen in groups of two to six. It is also quite common to see varieties of parrotfishes, pairs of filefishes, large spider crabs, southern stingrays and solitary barracuda.

Although 60 feet (18 m) is the maximum depth on this dive, it is a good first dive for photographers because most of the best

subjects are found close to the bottom. If done as a second dive, bottom time would be very limited.

19. LA FRANCESA REEF

DEPTH: 40-65 FEET

                (12-20 M)

CURRENT: MODERATE

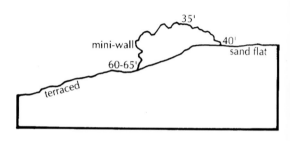

La Francesa Reef (The French Lady) is a long, wide reef on the shore side of the drop-off between the north end of Palancar Reef and the south end of Santa Rosa Reef. There is a flat sand bottom about 40 feet (12 m) deep on the shore side. The reef itself is approximately 50 to 70 feet (15-21 m) wide in most places, and rises very little above the level of the sandy bottom on the shore side.

On the offshore side of the reef, there is a small wall that descends steeply to a gently sloping sand and rubble bottom approximately 60 to 65 feet (18-20 m) deep. From there the

Black grouper are among the largest marine animals that divers usually encounter.

Large spider crabs are a common sight in tunnels and recesses.

Christmas tree tube worms are found on all the reefs.

bottom terraces down to the lip of the drop-off. There are a few sand channels completely separating sections of the reef, but most of the reef is continuous and unbroken.

Lots of cuts, overhangs and caves can be found here. Small branches of black coral hang from the ceilings of caves and tunnels. Queen angelfish, cowfish and various types of filefishes are very common at this site. Usually, a few small schools of French grunts and blue-striped grunts are tucked under the overhangs. The reef surface is thickly adorned with colorful sponges.

20. DALILA REEF

DEPTH:	25-80 FEET
	(8-24 M)
CURRENT:	MODERATE TO
	STRONG

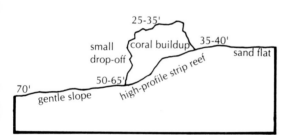

Dalila is a strip reef with a small drop-off or mini-wall that continues in a northerly direction from the north end of Palancar Shallows. The reef is named after the nearby Dalila Ranch. Dalila is actually a series of strip reef sections, separated by wide sandy channels. The sand bottom averages between 45 and 65 feet (14-20 m), but drops to as deep as 80 feet (24 m) in some places. Therefore, it is important to watch your depth, especially if you are on the second dive of the day. At the south end there are many caves, overhangs and cuts. The reef gets shallower as you move to the north. In places, the top of the reef comes to within 25 feet (8 m) of the surface.

Large vase sponges are commonly seen along most of the drop-offs.

Large friendly grouper. The first thing one notices at Dalila is the presence of many large, friendly grouper. The groupers never stray very far from the divers. In fact, they will often appear unexpectedly, cruising effortlessly across your path or turning, with seeming indifference, directly in front of you when you least expect it.

This reef is will known as a good place to explore for large, fat, green moray eels. They can usually be found tucked into and under low-lying ledges at the bottom of the coral heads. Some of these eels measure up to seven feet (2.1 m) in length.

A colony of tube worms filters the water for drifting plankton.

Dalila Reef offers a multitude of small invertebrates to photograph or videotape. This star-eyed hermit is a typical resident of the reef.

If the current is strong, and you don't spend much time poking around in the lee of the coral heads, you will come to the end of the reef in an area that is between the south ends of La Francesa and Paso Del Cedral. Both of these reefs begin at a depth of about 35 feet (11 m). Here you will encounter whitespotted filefish and scrawled filefish. If you observe these fish over a period of time and try to get close to them, you will notice that they are usually found in pairs, as are gray angelfish and French angelfish. The larger fish is presumably the male. Divers will usually find more queen angelfish in this area than on many of the reefs in Cozumel. Most of the coral heads, especially the brain corals, are covered with unusually large Christmas tree tube worms.

The reef is a very good site for photography and video, although it is not chosen as a first dive site very often because of its proximity to Palancar and Columbia. It is a little too deep for a second dive. It requires a longer surface interval and you have to spend this interval without being able to use the time to motor back north toward your resort. Therefore, diving here as a second site puts you back at your resort much later in the day. The varied marine life and colorful sponges make this reef a favorite with many photographers.

Southern stingrays frequent the shallow sandy areas inshore of Palancar Shallows (Palancar Gardens).

PALANCAR REEF (SITES 21-23)

Palancar Reef is the reef that is most often identified with Cozumel. It is actually a conglomeration of a number of different sections of reef that extend over three miles along the southwestern edge of the island. These sections are about a mile offshore, and offer a variety of structures and configurations.

21. PALANCAR SHALLOWS

DEPTH:	15-70 FEET
	(5-21 M)
CURRENT:	USUALLY LIGHT

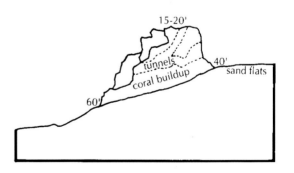

This site is also called Palancar Gardens and is located inside of and parallel to the entire length of the Palancar drop-off. At the northern end, Palancar Shallows is a strip reef, with a small drop-off of the offshore side of the reef. The inside of the reef is a flat sandy bottom in 40 feet (12 m) of water.

At the south end of Palancar Shallows, the reef structure rises only slightly above the sand bottom on its shore side. The reef then extends continuously to the Palancar Caves drop-off where the gently sloping sand and rubble bottom is between 60 and 70 feet (18-21 m) deep. As you swim farther to the north, the sand bottom on the shore side of the reef gets gradually shallower until reaching depths of 20 to 25 feet (6-8 m). In places, the top of the reef structure rises to within 15 to 25 feet (5-8 m) of the surface.

This interesting reef is between 40 and 80 feet (12-24 m) in width in most places, and is full of caves, overhangs and cuts. The northern part of Palancar Shallows is located on the inside of the northern end of the Palancar Reef area. This long, narrow section of reef has extensive cuts and valleys, with lots of finger canyons and tunnels penetrating the formation. The ceilings of most caves and tunnels are crowded with bright orange rope sponges and various types of algae. There are many massive pinnacles on the outer edges of the reef. On the walls of the interior cuts, there are many medium-sized, deep-water gorgonians extending into these openings.

In the summer and early fall, massive schools of silversides may be found flowing throughout the tunnels and caves in this area.

Divers will find only a few sea fans, but lots of whip corals and brain corals. Queen angelfish are plentiful, as are French and grey angels. Cleaning stations, mostly manned by juvenile hogfish, can be found everywhere around the reef. Cowfish, three-foot (1 m) barracuda, and schools of chubs and creole wrasse are common. The northern end of Palancar Shallows has greater numbers of tropical fishes.

22. PALANCAR HORSESHOE

DEPTH:	30-100+ FEET
	(9-30+ M)
CURRENT:	MODERATE

The Horseshoe is one of the most popular places to begin a drift dive at Palancar. This area was so named because of the large U-shaped cut in the reef structure. The top of the

"U" is at the drop-off, with the bottom of the "U" cut into the reef and pointing toward shore. The top of the reef around the horseshoe is approximately 30 feet (9 m) deep, and falls to about 65 feet (20 m) at the outside edges of the base. In 1985, a solid bronze, modernistic sculpture of Christ, measuring over 13 feet (4 m) in height, was placed here on a massive cubic base. When Hurricane Gilbert roared through the island in 1988, it knocked over the statue, which was then moved to Chankanaab. The hurricane filled in much of the horseshoe with sand. Today, a lot of the sand has been swept away by the ever-present currents, and the base of the statue is exposed. Where once the bottom of the horseshoe was flat, it now has a sloping bottom. This dive is usually done as a 60- to 80-foot (18-24 m) dive. As you follow the reef to the north of the horseshoe, you will find a labyrinth of caves, tunnels and passageways throughout the reef structure. There are still some large gorgonian fans, although there is not too much fish life except for schools of creole wrasse, chubs, angelfishes and yellowtail snapper. These fishes will follow groups of divers as they explore the spectacular terrain. Other schooling fishes that are occasionally seen here are ocean triggers and horse-eye jacks. Spent air percolates up through the top of the reef forming a wall of bubbles rising along the route divers follow inside the reef. The outside wall drops vertically to a steep rubble slope, beginning at a depth of about 100 feet (30 m). Perhaps the most interesting section of reef is just south of the horseshoe. At the end of the dive, as you are drifting over the shallows, keep an eye out for turtles. Small hawksbill and green sea turtles seem accustomed to the presence of divers and make great photo and video subjects.

Large Nassau groupers are often seen in and around the horseshoe near Palancar drop-off. These friendly groupers will often patiently pose for photographers.

Trumpetfish will frequently orient themselves to blend in with corals and sponges.

Queen angelfish are becoming very abundant on most reefs. Although usually skittish in many destinations, they are often cooperative as photo subjects in Cozumel.

23. PALANCAR CAVES

DEPTH:	20-100+ FEET
	(6-30+ M)
CURRENT:	LIGHT TO
	MODERATE

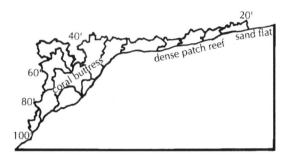

Palancar Caves is the area of Palancar Reef located south of the horseshoe. This site actually covers a distance of between two to three miles (1.2-1.9 km) of reef so it is impossible to see all of the Palancar Caves in only a few trips. In most places, the bottom on the shore side of the reef consists of flat, pure white sand with depths ranging from 30 to 40 feet (9-12 m). However, the reef structure occasionally extends into the shallows, joining with the southern part of Palancar Shallows. In some places, the sand bottom on the inside of the reef is only 20 feet (6 m) deep. However, the sand channel that separates Palancar Caves from Palancar Shallows dips to between 40 and 60 feet (12-18 m).

The broad reef structure of Palancar Caves is honeycombed with an extensive network of caves, tunnels, and pinnacles with intermittent sand falls and channels. The outside of the reef drops vertically to a steeply sloping sand and rubble drop-off that begins at about 100 feet (30 m). Most dive operations set maximum depth limits to 90 feet (27 m). The dive guides will then escort divers slowly up to shallower depths between 30 and 40 feet (9-12 m) to finish the dive on top of the reef or out over the sand. Look for southern rays, turtles and permit jacks as you finish your dive.

Schools of friendly and aggressive gray chubs and yellowtail snapper greet divers as they enter the water. Divers will find a few large deep water gorgonian fans protruding from the sides of the cuts in the coral. Small pinnacles, 30 or 40 feet (9-12 m) in height, are spaced at irregular intervals along the outside edge of the drop-off. There are also lots of encrusting sponges on the reef. Large groupers are frequently seen in this area.

Although there are not many schooling fishes in this area, there are a large number of unusual fishes, including trunkfishes, cowfishes, puffers, spotted drums, filefishes and hamlets.

The currents generally run from the south to the north and are usually light to moderate in strength. The south end of Palancar Caves is often referred to as "Palancar Bricks". The highlights of this area are beautiful pinnacles, some rising 60 or 70 feet (18-21 m). The dives are normally limited to 90 feet (27 m). Divers will usually encounter several hawksbill or green sea turtles in the shallows.

Encounters with hawksbill turtles are a common occurrence at Palancar Caves.

24. COLUMBIA GARDENS

DEPTH:	5-25 FEET
	(2-8 M)
CURRENT:	LIGHT TO
	MODERATE

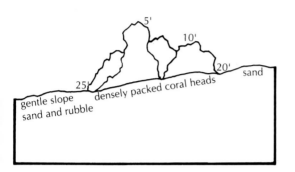

Columbia Gardens is a shallow reef that parallels the shoreline on the inside of the main reef. The relatively flat bottom which rarely dips below 25 feet (8 m) is sand and rubble. The reef is made up of a continuous string of large, high-profile coral heads, some of which come to within a few feet of the surface. Because of the shallow depth, this area makes an excellent second dive site to complement a wall dive at Maracaibo, Punta Sur or the Columbia Pinnacles.

This site is a beautiful area, teeming with marine life. Almost every type of tropical fish that is common to Cozumel can be found here. Keep an eye on the wide sandy area on either side of the reef where southern rays can often be seen feeding on shellfish. Even large loggerhead turtles have been spotted here.

Beautiful anemones form part of the tapestries of color on Cozumel's deep reefs.

25. COLUMBIA PINNACLES

DEPTH:	15-110+ FEET
	(5-33+ M)
CURRENT:	MODERATE TO
	STRONG
LEVEL:	EXPERIENCED

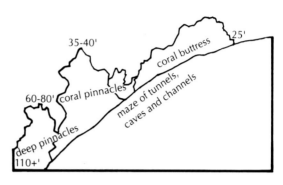

The Columbia Pinnacles is located between the south end of Palancar Reef and Punta Sur Reef. This Columbia Reef site has an impressive drop-off combined with spectacular massive pinnacles that rise from very deep water to within 60 to 110 feet (18-33 m) of the surface.

There is an extensive buildup of coral that begins in water 20 to 40 feet (6-12 m) deep. This coral buildup rises as it continues out toward the edge of the wall. The top of the formations come within 15 feet (5 m) of the surface in some places. The coral growth follows the contour of the slope into deeper water and becomes more extensive at the actual drop-off.

Steeply sloping sand channels wind in and around sections of the reef. The top of the main reef itself ranges in depth from 70 to 90 feet (21-27 m). Dive guides usually limit divers to a depth of 85 to 90 feet (26-27 m).

Often, divers encounter large grouper, turtles and eagle rays while winding over and around the spectacular formations. For the sheer majesty of the terrain, this area is unbeatable. In the blue expanse, divers will find large schools of yellow tailed snapper, horse-eye jacks, Bermuda chubs, Creole wrasse, and a wide variety of the other jacks. This is a great place to spot large fish. At certain times of the year, eagle rays and schools of small blacktip sharks appear at Columbia and have been known to frequent the same area for weeks at a time.

Caution. Because of the depths and currents, this area is recommended for experienced divers.

The drop-off near the mouth of a tunnel at Columbia Reef offers spectacular scenery.

26. PUNTA SUR REEF

DEPTH:	80-130+ FEET [24-42+ M]
CURRENT:	OFTEN STRONG
LEVEL:	EXPERIENCED

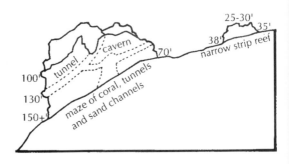

Punta Sur Reef is a deep wall dive located to the south of Columbia Reef just off Punta Sur (South Point). The top of the wall is approximately 80 to 100 feet (24-30 m) deep. It is the farthest south of the reefs that have massive coral buildup at and over the lip of the drop-off. This area is honeycombed with incredible caverns and tunnels carved in the wall mostly at depths between 80 and 140 feet (24-42 m).

Fabulous tunnel complex. Punta Sur offers the largest underwater rooms and chambers that can be found in Cozumel, and a fabulous complex of interconnecting tunnels and mysterious dead-end caves. Vertical columns and windows to the interior create spectacular lighting effects inside the reef. Some operations have begun to refer to part of this area as the Cathedral. At one point, there is a vertical tunnel aptly named Devil's Throat, which can be entered at 100 feet (30 m) and exited at 130 feet (39 m).

A pair of sponges and a gorgonian are examined by a diver on the wall at Punta Sur.

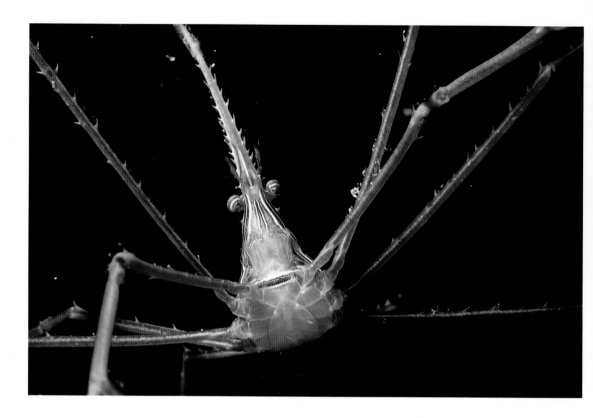

Arrow crabs are found almost
everywhere you look on the
shallow reefs of Cozumel.

Pufferfish (balloonfish) will ingest
water to cause their bodies to
expand and their spines to protrude
at right angles from their bodies.
This is done as a defense
mechanism to discourage predators.

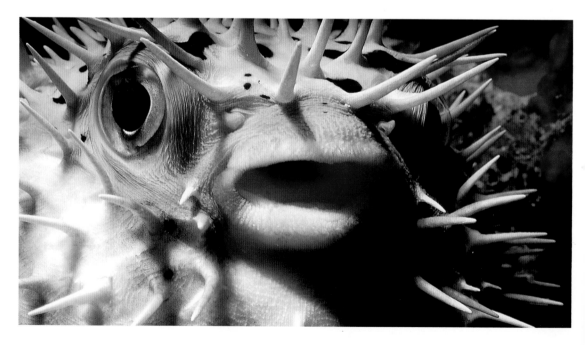

Bright red, deep-water gorgonians are very common throughout the Punta Sur Reef area.

Scorpionfish are masters of disguise and camouflage.

Fishes are not abundant at this site, although turtles, large angels and squirrelfishes are common. There is a fair chance that divers will see nurse sharks in the caves, and rays feeding in the sand or flying by along the drop-off. Most of the caverns and tunnels have sandy bottoms, so be sure to control buoyancy as you make your way through the tunnels and caverns. The ceiling of most caves, tunnels, and overhangs are covered with a jumble of orange and purple rope sponges.

This is an advanced boat dive. Dive profiles are set so that the maximum depth is a minimum of 110 feet (33 m). Before dive guides take groups to this area, they need to be assured of diver skill levels.

Inside the drop-off at Punta Sur, there is a shallow strip reef on a flat sandy bottom that lies in about 35 feet (11 m) of water. This area is usually referred to as Punta Sur Shallows.

27. MARACAIBO REEF

DEPTH:	80-130+ FEET
	[18-39+ M]
CURRENT:	OFTEN STRONG
LEVEL:	EXPERIENCED

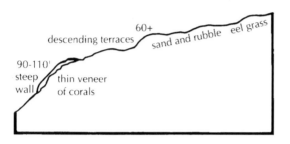

Maracaibo Reef is one of the two southernmost dive sites on the island.

Maracaibo consists of reef terraces extending outward from the southeastern point of the island. There are three separate sections of reef located just offshore from Punta Celarain (Point Celarain), within sight of the Point Celarain Lighthouse. The tops of these reef terraces range from 60 to 120 feet (18-36 m), getting deeper as you get closer to the actual drop-off. The lip of the drop-off slopes gradually deeper as you move farther away from Point Celarain. When you go over the edge of the wall, the drop-off begins with a steep slope between 90 and 120 feet (27-36 m). A sheer vertical wall with some undercuts starts between 130 and 150 feet (39-45 m).

Caution. Maracaibo is strictly a boat dive which should be left to experienced divers who can deal with strong, variable currents and extreme depths. Because of the depth, no-decompression bottom time is limited to only a few minutes. All divers should do a three- to five- minute safety stop at 15 feet (5 m). If

A photographer cruises through a tunnel on Cozumel's barrier reef.

Schools of blue tang will swim above the reef and then, as if on a prearranged signal, will stop in unison to feed for a few minutes in the same location.

divers go over the limits and require decompression stops, they will be forced to conduct them while drift diving in open ocean. For this reason, it is important for all divers in a group to stay together so that the boat captain can keep close track of the entire group. The next stop after the south point of Cozumel is a long way off.

Caution. Descend close to the edge of the drop-off because currents can be strong and unpredictable. While currents usually run parallel to the reef, they frequently run away from the drop-off towards the shallows. Sometimes there is even a down current over the wall. If you drop to the bottom away from the lip, you may have to kick hard or pull yourself along the bottom to get to the drop-off, wasting precious air, time and energy. The top of the reef is generally flat with sand, rubble, and scattered coral heads. There are a few areas with some interesting caves and tunnels along the wall. However, the wall itself in most areas within recommended sport diving depth limits is not very interesting.

Large pelagics. The real attraction offered here is the chance to encounter large pelagics. Because of the many divers who visit Cozumel, most large animals stay away from the more popular reefs. Eagle rays, sharks and schools of jacks are now only found in the more remote areas such as Maracaibo. Large groupers, weighing up to 200 pounds (91 kg) and measuring five feet (2 m) in length, and huge loggerhead sea turtles are also commonly seen at Maracaibo.

Maracaibo shallows. The higher terraces at Maracaibo are much shallower toward Point Celarain. The bottom along some of these terraces is in the 50- to 60-foot (15-18 m) range. In this area, you will find many large coral heads and a variety of deep-water corals. Schools of grunts and snapper are usually present, and divers will frequently encounter nurse sharks crammed inside small crevices.

Large solitary barracuda are often seen cruising over the reef at night hunting for food.

LESS FREQUENTED SITES

The sites listed below are either seldom visited by dive boats, or are for very experienced divers and require prior arrangements.

28. CANTARELL REEF

29. BARRACUDA REEF

30. SAN JUAN REEF

DEPTH:	60-80 FEET (18-24 M)
CURRENT:	STRONG TO VERY STRONG
LEVEL:	VERY EXPERIENCED

Colorful rope sponges form part of the beautiful mosaic on the island's southern reefs.

These reefs are located at the drop-off along the north end of San Miguel, on the northwestern end of the island. Dives at these reefs require making prior arrangements with a dive operator and must be cleared through the harbor master's office. Only a few operations visit these sites. Trips are limited to no more than six divers and all divers must be very experienced. The currents are usually very strong and unpredictable in this area.

All three areas offer fairly flat, strip reefs in the 60- to 80-foot (18-24 m) depth range. The back reef is sand, rubble and small coral heads in most places, with a very slight slope. The main incentive for diving these areas is the chance to see large animals. Schools of jacks, rays, sharks, barracuda and other pelagics are very common. The terrain is more uneven at the San Juan site where the reef ends in a large, natural bowl. Jacks often congregate here. From early December through March, schools of eagle rays are frequently seen along the drop-off. Schools of 30 to 50 eagle rays are not uncommon. During this time of year, many operations will run special afternoon trips to look for the eagle rays. Green moray eels, large lobster, and immense sponges are typically seen at the edge of the drop-off. Southern rays shadowed by bar jacks are common on the sand and nurse sharks are frequently discovered.

Pelagic animals, such as this gray reef shark, are often encountered on advanced current dives at such locations as Barracuda Reef and San Juan Reef. Permission from the harbor master and advanced diving skills are required to visit these sites.

31. CARDONA REEF

DEPTH:	20-30 FEET
	(6-9 M)
CURRENT:	LIGHT

Cardona Reef is a shallow, low profile strip reef to the south of Cardona Point. The reef is located just offshore where the bottom averages 25 to 30 feet (8-9 m). This area is usually used as a beach dive or for snorkeling. The reef ridge rises an average of 15 to 26 feet (5-8 m) above the bottom, and has many ledges and overhangs. The site was named after Rene Cardona Sr., who was the producer of the first movie filmed in Cozumel, Mundo Nuevo (New World).

The reef is visited more regularly as a beginner dive or second dive by the boat operations serving the southern hotels.

On many reefs, squirrelfishes can be found in almost every hole and crevice.

A spotted eagle ray cruises along the drop-off at San Juan Reef.

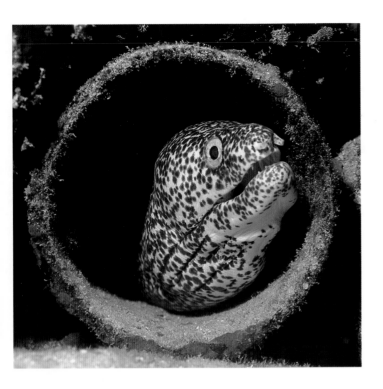

A spotted moray eel keeps a wary eye on divers from the protection of a pipe protruding from an artificial reef in front of Scuba Club Cozumel.

32. PALANCAR DEEP

DEPTH:	20-30 FEET
	(6-9 M)
CURRENT:	LIGHT

Palancar Deep is located at the south end of Palancar Reef, just to the north of Columbia Pinnacles. The top of the reef averages 60 feet (18 m). There is a steep vertical wall here with a massive coral structure and an extensive network of tunnels and caves. This is generally a great place to encounter turtles, schools of jacks and ocean triggers, as well as the occasional black-tip reef shark. There large numbers of southern rays feeding on the back reef, which is comprised mostly of sand flats.

Sponges provide a colorful part of the surface area on the healthy reefs of Cozumel.

33. CHUN CHACAAB

DEPTH:	10-120+ FEET
	(3-36+ M)
CURRENT:	STRONG

Chun Chacaab Reef is a wall southwest of Punta Celarain, between Maracaibo Reef and Punta Sur Reef. There is a wide sand fall between Punta Sur Reef and Chun Chacaab that slopes steeply to 120 feet (36 m), before ending in a vertical drop-off. The lip of the drop-off, which has little coral buildup, is at approximately 100 feet (30 m). This site is seldom visited by dive boats.

On the shore side of the drop-off is a vast, gently sloping, sand and rubble bottom that extends outward from the beach between Columbia Lagoon and Punta Celarain. The bottom is typically covered with grasses and occasional small coral heads and sponges. Conch shells are very common in this area. Dolphins are frequently seen cavorting in the shallows and feeding upon the plentiful shellfish found here.

CHAPTER **VII** MARINE LIFE

Cozumel has a wonderful assortment of colorful, interesting and unusual marine life awaiting the visiting diver.

Although there are only a few potentially harmful animals, and these are not normally aggressive, divers should still be cautious as to what they touch. Most of the animals mentioned in the following sections are abundant in Cozumel waters.

INTERESTING OR UNUSUAL FISHES

Angelfishes

Cozumel has three predominant species of angelfishes that are commonly found throughout the reefs which run along the west coast of the island. Although there are several other species of angelfishes, the **French angelfish**, the **gray angelfish** and the **queen angelfish** are the most commonly seen.

The **gray angelfish**, (*Pomacanthus arcuatus*), like the French angelfish is almost always found in pairs. Its color is uniformly gray to grayish-brown. It has a white mouth and the inner surface of the pectoral fin is yellow. This species is usually the least timid of the large angels and will often approach and sometimes swim slow circles around divers. Its maximum size is 18 to 20 inches (46-51 cm).

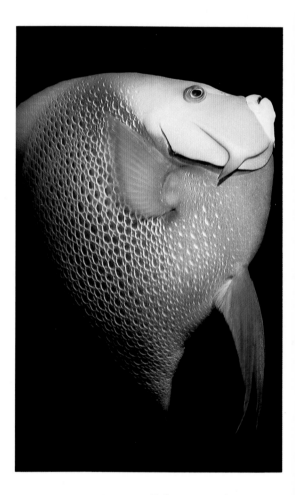

Gray angelfish (Pomacanthus arcuatus).

Swarms of silversides or baitfish are often seen flowing through the various chambers of the underground caves.

French angelfish (Pomacanthus paru).

The **French angelfish** (*Pomacanthus paru*) is predominantly black with its crescent shaped scales edged in bright yellow. It also has a white mouth and eyes that are ringed in bright yellow. The French angelfish is usually found in pairs and will occasionally approach divers. Its maximum size is 18 inches (46 cm).

The **queen angelfish** (*Holacanthus ciliaris*) is predominantly royal blue with yellow rims on the scales, and yellow pectoral, ventral and tail fins. Its face is usually yellow, with blue lips and a dark blue "crown" ringed in light blue on its forehead. Queen angelfish are generally shy and often are found in groups of three to six. Its average size is 8 to 14 inches (20-36 cm) with a maximum of 18 inches (46 cm).

Queen angelfish (Holacanthus ciliaris).

Balloonfish

The primary color of the **balloonfish** or **spiny puffer** (*Diodon holocanthus*) is usually tan to mottled brown, often with dark blotches. The pupil of the eye is an iridescent blue-green. This fish usually swims close to the reef or along rubble bottoms, blending in with the background. They will inflate with water when molested or threatened, resulting in a dramatic increase in size, and causing sharp spines that cover their body to project outward. Their average size is 8 to 14 inches (20-46 cm).

Balloonfish (Diodon holocanthus).

Honeycomb cowfish (Lactophrys polygonia).

Cowfishes

There are two species of cowfish found in Cozumel, the **honeycomb cowfish** (*Lactophrys polygonia*) and the **scrawled cowfish** (*Lactophrys quadricornis*). The primary color of the cowfish varies from blue to green. The honeycomb cowfish has a pattern that resembles a honeycomb. Both species have a sharp spine above each eye. Their maximum length is 18 inches (46 cm).

This fish is extremely shy and will avoid divers. They rely on camouflage to hide from predators.

Longsnout Sea Horse

The **longsnout sea horse** *(Hippocampus reidi)*, while still fairly rare, is now found more often on the shallow offshore reefs. Its color is variable, from yellow to brown or reddish-brown. While this species is very similar to the lined seahorse, it can be distinguished by the presence of tiny black spots on the head and body. This remarkable little animal anchors itself by wrapping its tail around sea rods, branches of gorgonians and sea grasses.

Longsnout sea horse (Hippocampus reidi).

Splendid toadfish (Sanopus splendidus).

Splendid Toadfish

The **splendid toadfish** (*Sanopus splendidus*) is one of two species of toadfish found in Cozumel. It is believed that the splendid toadfish, also called the "Cozumel catfish," is not found anywhere else in the Caribbean. This distinctive fish has a wide compressed head with whisker like appendages growing from its lower jaw. It has horizontal striping and some mottling, usually with charcoal gray or brownish gray lines over white. It has a bright yellow border on all of its primary fins. It grows to a length of 12 inches (31 cm).

The toadfish is commonly seen peering from the entrance of low crevices, perched on its pectoral or ventral fins. These crevices are most likely to be on sand and rubble bottoms along the sides of shallow and medium-deep strip reefs, or under coral heads closer to shore. At night when it is more active, you can often hear its low guttural mating call reverberating through the water.

Spotted Drum

The **spotted drum** (*Equetus punctatus*) is easily distinguishable as it has black and white bars on the head, and several stripes on the body. The rear dorsal and tail fin are black with white spots. Its maximum length is 10 inches (26 cm). This fish is unafraid of divers and can often be observed repeating circular or figure-eight swimming patterns. The juvenile has an extremely long dorsal fin.

Spotted drum (Equetus punctatus).

Trumpetfish (Aulostomus maculatus).

Trumpetfish

The **trumpetfish** (*Aulostomus maculatus*) has a long, thin body. Its usual color phase is brown to reddish-brown, but it can also be seen as silver or yellow. It can often be seen in a head down position, camouflaging themselves by mimmicking stalks of sea rods. Their average size is 18 to 30 inches (46-76 cm). Their maximum size is 3 feet (1 m).

Whitespotted Filefish

The **whitespotted filefish** (*Cantherhines macroceros*) has two distinct color phases. In one color phase, the body color is almost orangish or yellowish brown; in the other color phase the body is covered with white spots. This fish commonly ranges about the reef in what are believed to be mated pairs. Usually there is one of each color phase within the pair. They average 10 to 15 inches (26-38 cm) in size reaching a maximum of 18 inches (46 cm).

Whitespotted filefish (Cantherhines macroceros).

Interesting or Unusual Invertebrates

Christmas Tree Tube Worm

Feathered **Christmas tree tube worms** (*Spirobranchus giganteus*) are usually found on the surface of boulders or brain corals. They can appear in a myriad of colors including orange, red, maroon, blue, brown or yellow. They are worms whose tubes are embedded deeply inside the coral, so that only the expanded colorful branchiae are visible.

These worms sense changes in pressure and light, and will instantly retract into their tubes for protection. The spirobranchus has two diagonally projecting "Christmas trees," each with four to six whorls (or levels), which decrease in diameter as they get closer to the top.

Christmas tree tube worm (Spirobranchus giganteus).

Flamingo tongue cowrie (Cyphoma gibbosum).

Flamingo Tongue Cowrie

Flamingo tongue cowries (*Cyphoma gibbosum*) prey upon polyps of various corals, such as the purple sea fan. The cowrie inserts its proboscis into the cups and rasps away the living tissue with its rasp-like tongue called a radula. Unless molested or otherwise threatened, the flamingo tongue cowrie displays its orange and black mantle, which closely resembles the spots of a leopard. It is believed that this cowrie is so brazen about displaying its mantle because it is a major factor in ensuring reproduction. When the mantle is retracted, the outside of the shell has a pinkish-white to orangish-white tint.

Rock Mantis Shrimp

The common **rock mantis shrimp** (*Squilla empusu*) can be found in tiny recesses or caves in the limestone bottom in shallow offshore areas. Mantis shrimp have a razor-sharp finger, so divers should be careful about poking fingers down their dens. Their color varies from dark mottled green, to yellow-green or black. They can reach a maximum length of 4 inches (10 cm).

Rock mantis shrimp (Squilla empusa).

Hermit crab (Dardanus venosus).

Hermit Crab

Star-eyed **hermit crabs** (*Dardanus venosus*) can easily be recognized by the corneas of its eyes which are greenish-blue in color. They also have a dark central spot and radiating lines forming a star pattern. The maximum size of the carapace is slightly over 1 inch (2.6 mm) in diameter. Hermit crabs move their homes from shell to shell. As they outgrow the old one they look for a larger home that has been deserted.

Reef Squid

Reef squid (*Sepioteuthis sepioidea*) have fins that begin just behind the mouth and run the length of their body. These fins employ a rippling movement used to aid in propulsion. They swim with their short tentacles bunched, and are usually seen in groups of six to eight, moving slowly in shallow areas near shore. Their maximum length is about a foot (31 cm).

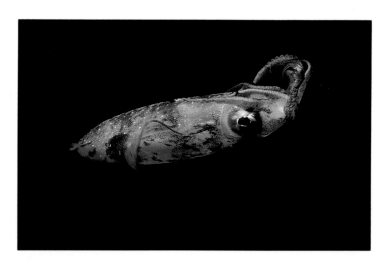

Reef squid (Sepioteuthis sepioidea).

Rough file clam (Lima scabra).

Rough File Clam

The **rough file clam** (*Lima scabra*) is a small, nondescript cream to brown colored shell. However, when the shell opens up, it displays a beautiful orange or red animal that extends long, streaming tentacles. The maximum length of the shell is approximately 3 inches (8 cm).

Bristle Worms

Two polychaete (many-bristled) worms, the **fire worm** (*Hermodice carunculata*) and the **red-tipped fire worm** (*Chloeia viridis*), are lined with thousands of glassy, needle-like bristles. At the slightest contact with the skin, the bristles penetrate and break off, causing inflammation, itching and numbness. The fire worm is particularly common on the reefs. They grow to about 10 inches (26 cm).

Fire worm (Hermodice carunculata).

Fire Coral

The encrusting **fire coral** (*Millepora complanata*) is only one type of fire coral that exists on the reefs in Cozumel. It forms branching colonies. The coloration of most fire corals is usually a light brown or tan with white tips or edges. Upon close inspection, you can usually discern microscopic polyps which extend from pinhole-sized cups. Contact with any of the fire corals produces painful welts.

Eels

The **spotted moray** (*Gymnothorax moringa*) is the most common moray eel found in Cozumel. It has a white body with black spots or blotches all over its body. The spotted moray is also primarily a nocturnal feeder. It reaches a length of about 5 feet (1.5 m).

Morays are normally not a threat to divers. However, morays that are used to being fed by guides, will often come all the way out of the reef to search for morsels of food when divers approach. Morays have very bad eyesight and seek food using their sense of smell, which sometimes leads to fingers being mistakenly bitten. Divers should never stick their hands into holes in the reef. This may also lead to a nip by a defensive moray.

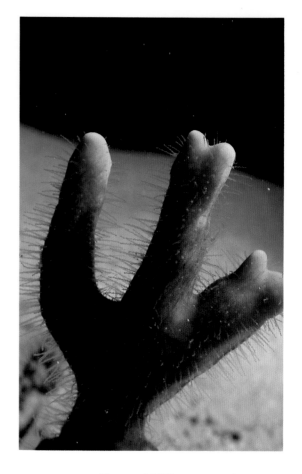

Fire coral (Millepora complanata).

Spotted moray (Gymnothorax moringa).

The **green moray** (*Gymnothorax funebris*) is the largest species of moray eel found in Cozumel. It has a uniform green or greenish-brown color. The moray is a nocturnal hunter. It receives a reputation for being viscious because it constantly opens and closes its mouth, not as a threat but simply to pass water over its gills. They can grow to a length of 7 feet (2.1 m).

Spiny Sea Urchins

The long-spined **black sea urchin** (*Diadema antillarum*) is normally nocturnal. During the day, they hide in reef crevices or aggregate in groups on the shallow bottom. At night these animals scatter over the sea floor, feeding on algae and turtle grass. Full grown adults are usually black. In younger specimens the color may be banded brown and black, or white and brown. The long spines of these animals contain toxins and can cause excruciating pain if the tips of the spines penetrate and break off under the skin.

Long-spined black sea urchin (Diadema antillarum).

Green moray (Gymnothorax funebris).

Spotted scorpionfish (Scorpaena plumieri).

Spotted Scorpionfish

The **spotted scorpionfish** (*Scorpaena plumieri*) is a master of disguise. It is actually quite common, but rarely seen because it blends in well with a sand and rubble bottom and will not move unless molested. Its color is usually gray to light brown. The only time the fish is easy to spot is when it swims, exposing the top of its pectoral fins, that are banded in reddish brown, orange, black and yellow. Some specimens may grow to 18 inches (46 cm) in length. They are frequently found in pairs. These bottom dwelling rockfish have the ability to inject poison through the spines in their dorsal, anal and pelvic fins.

Yellow Stingray

The **yellow stingray** (*Urolophus jamaicensis*) has a smallish, yellow-brown body covered with blotches and spots. It has a tail with a venomous spine, that can inflict a painful sting. This ray is usually found on sand and rubble bottoms. Divers should avoid trying to grab or otherwise molest this animal which reaches a length of about 15 inches (38 cm).

Yellow stingray (Urolophus jamaicensis).

APPENDIX 1

EMERGENCY NUMBERS

Recompression Chambers

Sub-Aquatic Safety Services   **22387**
                     VHF Channel 6

Buceo Medico Mexicano   **22387**
24-Hour Emergency number   **21430**
                VHF Channels 16 & 21
Calle 5 Sur #21 B
E-Mail: Servicios@cozunet.finred.com.mx
Bi-Lingual Hyperbaric Certified Physicians.
Full no cost coverage if $1.00/day prepaid
dive insurance obtained prior to diving.
Double lock, 54-inch two-person hyperbaric
chamber.

Cozumel Hyperbaric Research
24-Hour Emergency number   **23070**
                    VHF Channel 65
Dr. Pascual Piccolo
San Miguel Medical Clinic
Calle 6 #132 (bet. 5th & 10th Av.)
E-Mail: Meditur@cozumel.czm.com.mx
Full no cost coverage if $1.00/day prepaid
dive insurance obtained prior to diving.
Modern, state of the art, double lock, 60"
multi-person hyperbaric chamber.

Hospital   20140

Ambulance   20639

Police   20092

Doctors

Listed below is a selection of English speaking
doctors. Your hotel will be glad to recommend
additional doctors or dentists.

M.F. Lewis, M.D.   **21616/20912**
50 bis #840, Bet. 11th & 13th Street
American
General practice

Carlos Peniche, M.D.   **21319/22919**
20 Av. Norte #425
24-hour service

Gynecology, fractures, pediatrics, trauma,
intestinal disorders, hospitalization

Ricardo Segovia, G.D.   **20714**
11 Av. Sur #101, Suite 2A
24-hour service
Gynecology, fractures, pediatrics, trauma,
intestinal disorders, hospitalization

Paulina Calderon, M.D.   **21440**
#181 Coldwell Av. at 30 Av.
24-hour service
General practice

Divers Alert Network (DAN)

The Divers Alert Network (DAN), a non-profit
membership organization operates a **24-hour**
Diving Emergency Hotline number (919) 684-
8111 (dive emergencies only) to provide divers
and physicians with medical advice on
treating diving injuries. DAN also operates a
Dive Safety and Medical Information Line
from 8:30 A.M. to 5 P.M. EST for non-emergency
inquiries. DAN can also organize air
evacuation to a recompression chamber as
well as emergency medical evacuation for
non-dive-related injuries for members. Since
many emergency room physicians do not
know how to properly treat diving injuries, it
is highly recommended that in the event of an
accident, you have the physician consult a
DAN doctor specializing in diving medicine.

    All DAN members receive $100,000
emergency medical evacuation assistance and
a subscription to the magazine, *Alert Diver*.
New members receive the DAN Dive and
Travel Medical Guide and can buy up to
$250,000 of dive accident insurance. DAN
offers oxygen first-aid training, and provides
funding and consulting for recompression
chambers worldwide. They also conduct
diving research at Duke University Medical
Center's Center for Hyperbaric Medicine and
Environmental Physiology. DAN's address is 6
West Colony Place, Durham, NC 27705. To
join call (800) 446-2671 in the U.S. and
Canada or (919) 684-2948.

APPENDIX 2

USEFUL NUMBERS FOR VISITORS

Airlines

AeroCaribe   Cozumel 20928/20877
                         Cancun 41231/42000

AeroCozumel   Cozumel 20468
                         Cancun 41231/42000

Continental   Cozumel 20487/20576

Mexicana   Cozumel 20263/20157/20133

Airport Immigration   20516

Ferry   20861

Long Distance Operator

2 Av. 5 Calle Norte, near Calle 1 Sur.
(On the Plaza)
You can call direct or collect from most resort hotels. By calling collect you can save the 70 percent tax.

Port Captain   20169

Post Office   20106

Avenida Rafael Melgar at Calle 7 Sur
(4 blocks south of the Plaza)
Hours M-F 9 a.m. to 1 P.M., 3 to 6 P.M.;
Saturday 9 A.M. to 1 P.M.

Pharmacies

Farmacia Dori   20559
Adolfa Rosada Salas #20A

Los Portales   20741
Calle 11 Sur # 11

Farmacia Joaquin   20125
East side of the Plaza

Photo and Video Services

Blue Planet Custom Videos   24918
Camera rentals and professionally produced underwater videos of your trip

Cozumel Images   22238
                                Fax: 22238
Located in downtown San Miguel, ° block from the waterfront on Calle 2 between Rafael Melgar and 5th Av.
E-Mail: czi@cozumel.com.mx
Customized videos, editing services, underwater photo accessories, film processing, and underwater camera and housing rentals

Island Photo-Video Center   25833
                                Fax: 20065
Located at the entrance to the LaCeiba Hotel, south of San Miguel.
E-Mail: photocoz@cozumel.net
           alentado@cozumel.com.mx
Rental equipment, photography and video instruction, repairs, film processing and retail sales

APPENDIX 3

DIVE OPERATIONS

To telephone Cozumel from the United States add **011-52-987-87** before the five-digit local number.

Aldora Divers
Calle 5 Sur 37
Tel: 23397 Fax: 23397
E-Mail: jonge@aldora.com

Antonio Castellanos Eagle-Ray Divers
Tel: 25735 Fax: 68237
E-Mail: eagleray@cozumel.com.mx

Aqua Safari
39 Av. Melgar, San Miguel
Tel: 20101 Fax: 20661
E-Mail: dive@aquasafari.com.mx

Aqua World Cozumel
Carretera Sur Km 3.7, Playa Paraiso
Tel: 21210 Fax: 21210
E-Mail: agwssc@cozumel.com.mx

Blue Angel Scuba School
Located in front of the Villa Blanca Hotel
Tel: 21631 Fax: 20913
E-Mail: dive@aquasafari.com

Blue Bubble Divers
1. Corner of Calle 3 Sur & 5th Av.
2. Yucab Reef at Casa Del Mar Hotel
3. Dzul Ha Reef at Del Sol Hotel
Tel: 21865 Fax: 21865
E-Mail: bubbles@.cozunet.finred.com.mx

Buena Ventura Diving
Tel: 21774 Fax: 21774
E-Mail: ventural@cozumel.net

Caballito del Caribe
Tel: 21449 Fax: 21449
E-mail: cdcaribe@aol.com

Careyitos Advanced Divers
35 Av. Sur bet. 3 Sur & Morelos
Tel: 21578 Fax: 21417
E-Mail: careyitos@cozumel.czm.com.mx

Caribbean Divers
1. R.E. Melgar y 5 Sur (#415)
2. Chankanaab Underwater Park
3. Sol Cabanas del Caribe Hotel
Tel: 21145/21080 Fax: 21426
E-Mail: caridive@cozumel.com.mx

Cinpatica Charters
La Caleta next to El Presidente Hotel
Tel: 21817 Fax: 21817
E-Mail: felipeq@cozumel.com.mx

Cozumel Custom Aquatics
Located at Pro Dive, A.R. Salas #198 at 5th Av.
Tel: 25566 Fax: 25566

Cozumel Equalizers Scuba Center
Located at Adolfo Rosado Salas #72
Tel: 23511 Fax: 23511
E-Mail: darwin@cozumel.com.mx

Del Mar Aquatics
1. Casa Del Mar Hotel
2. La Ceiba Hotel
Tel: 25674/25949 Fax: 23532
E-Mail: delmaraq@cozumel.com.mx

Deportes Aquaticos
Located at the Plaza Las Garzas
Tel: 20640 Fax: 20640
E-Mail: aquatics@cozumel.com.mx

Dive House
1. South side of the main plaza bet. Av. Melgar & Av. 5th
2. At the Fiesta Americana Hotel
Tel: 21953 Fax: 23068
E-Mail: dive@divehouse.com

Dive Palancar
Located at the Allegro Resort
Tel: 25094/23443 Fax: 25094
E-Mail: divepal@cozunet.finred.com.mx

Dive Paradise
601 Av. Melgar, San Miguel
Tel: 21007 Fax: 21061
E-Mail: appledp@cozumel.com

David & Nancy's Sea Scuba
Juarez Av. bet. 10th Av. & 15th Av.
Tel: 23778 Fax: 23778
E-Mail: seascuba@cozumel.czn.com.mx

Dive With Martin
Tel: 22610 Fax: 21340

Diving Adventures
Calle 5 Sur #2 bet. Rafael Melgar & 5th Av.

Eco Divers
Located at 10th Av. & 19th Av. Sur
Tel: 25628 Fax: 25628
E-Mail: ecodivers@cozunet.finred.com.mx

Scuba Club Cozumel
Carretera Costera Sur Km 1.5
Tel: 20663 Fax: 20663
E-Mail:
scubacozumel@cozunet.finred.com.mx

Marine Sports
Hotel Fiesta Inn, Carretera Costera Sur Km 1.7
Tel: 25062 Fax: 22154
E-Mail: marinesp@cozumel.czm.com.mx

Mexico Diving Explorer
Calle 10 Norte #232 bet. 10th & 15th Av.

Tel: 25179 Fax: 20880
E-Mail: divemexico@cozumel.com.mx

Michelle's Dive Shop
5 Av. Sur #201 y A.R. Salas
Tel: 20947 Fax: 26488
E-Mail: dive@cozumel.com.mx

Papa Hog's Scuba Emporium
Carretera Costera Sur Km 2.85
Tel: 21651 Fax: 24465
E-Mail: diving@papahogs.com

Paul's Private Dive Center
Rafael Melgar & 11th St. Sur
Tel: 20141 Fax: 20141
E-Mail: pauls@cozunet.finred.com.mx

Pepe's Dive Shop
Coral Princess Hotel
Carretera Costera Norte Km 2.5
Tel: 23200 Fax: 22800

E-Mail: pepedive@cozumel.com.mx

Rosendo Espejel
Tel: 68180
E-Mail: rosendo@cozumel.net

Scuba Cozumel
Carretera Costera Sur Km 1.5
Tel: 20627 Fax: 21977
E-Mail:
scubacozumel@cozunet.finred.com.mx

Scuba Du Dive Center
1. Hotel Presidente Intercontinental
2. Calle 3 Sur #33 bet. waterfront & 5th Av.
Tel: 21994/20322 Fax: 24130
E-Mail: scubadu@cozumel.net

Snorkel Center & Diving
Tel: 26364 Fax: 26364
E-Mail: snorkcen@cozumel.com.mx

Scuba Shack
Carretera Costera Sur
Tel: 24240 Fax: 23836
E-Mail: scubas@cozumel.finred.com.mx

Staff Diver
100th Av. & Calle 1 Sur #99
Tel: 20755 Fax: 20755
E-Mail: staffczm@cozumel.com.mx

TTC Club Divers
Club Cozumel Caribe
Carretera Costera Norte Km 4.5
Tel: 24476 Fax: 24476
E-Mail: ttcdiving@ttcdiving.com

Wildcat Divers
5th Av. bet. 2 & 4 North
E-Mail: anoaat@cozunet.finred.com.mx

ANOAAT

The Cozumel Watersports & Tourism Assoc.
Tel: 25955 Fax: 25966
E-Mail: anoaat@cozunet.finred.com.mx

APPENDIX 4

HELPFUL WORDS AND PHRASES

General

I don't speak Spanish.	*No hablo Espanol.*
	(no ahb-low es-pan-yole)
I don't understand.	*No entiendo.*
	(no ent-e-yen-do)
How are you?	*Como esta usted?*
	(caw-mo es-tah oo-sted)
Very well, thank you.	*Muy bien, gracias.*
	(moo-ee be-yen, grahs-yas)
Come here, please.	*Venga aqui, por favor.*
	(veng-gah ah-key, poor fayvor)
What is your name?	*Como te llama?*
	(caw-mo tay yah-ma)
My name is...	*Me llamo...*
	(may yah-mo)
The bill please.	*La cuenta, por favor.*
	(lah kwen-tah por-fay-vor)
How much is it?	*Cuanto cuesta?*
	(kwen-toe kwess-tah)
One more	*Uno mas*
	(oo-no moss)
Hello/good day.	*Buenos dias.*
	(bway-nohss dee-ahss)
Thank you.	*Gracias.*
	(grah-see-ahs)
You're welcome.	*De nada.*
	(day nah-dah)
Goodbye.	*Adios.*
	(ah-day-ohss)
Yes.	*Si.*
	(see)
No.	*No.*
	(no)
Excuse me.	*Perdoneme.*
	(pair-dough-neh-may)
Where is...?	*Donde esta...?*
	(Doan-day ess-tah)
...a hotel?	*...un hotel?*
	(oon oh-tell)
...the toilet?	*...el bano?*
	(ell bahn-yoh)
...a good doctor?	*...un buen medico?*
	(oon bwayn may-dee-co)
When?	*Cuando?*
	(kwahn-do)
What?	*Que?*
	(kay)
Tomorrow	*Mañana*
	(mahn-yawn-ah)

Good	*Bueno*
	(bway-no)
Do you speak English?	*Habla usted Ingles?*
	(ab-la oo-sted ing-glace)
Two persons	*Dos personas*
	(dose pair-so-nahs)

Directions

Avenue	*Avenida*
Left	*Izquierda*
	(ees-ky-erh-day)
Right	*Derecha*
	(day-ray-chah)
North	*Norte*
South	*Sur*
Point	*Punta*
Street	*Calle*

Menu Terms

Beer	*Cerveza*
	(sir-vay-sah)
Bread	*Pan*
Cake	*Torta*
Coffee w/ cream	*Cafe con crema*
Coffee, black	*Cafe negro*
Chicken	*Pollo*
	(poi-yoh)
Eggs	*Huevos*
	(way-vohs)
Fried	*Frito*
Juice	*Jugo*
Ice	*Hielo*
	(he-ay-low)
Ice cream	*Helado*
Lobster	*Langosta*
Meat	*Carne*
Milk	*Leche*
	(letch-ay)
Roasted	*Asado*
Shrimp	*Camarones*
Soft drink	*Refresco*
Sugar	*Azucar*
Soup	*Sopa*
	(soap-ah)
Water	*Agua*
	(ag-wah)

INDEX

A **boldface** page number denotes a picture caption.
An <u>underlined</u> page number indicates detailed treatment.